Natural Bridge

A Journal of Contemporary Literature

Number 19 Spring 2008
University of Missouri–St. Louis

FOUNDING & SENIOR EDITOR
Steven Schreiner

GUEST EDITOR
Mary Troy

MANAGING EDITOR
Olivia Ayes

ASSISTANT EDITORS
Steven Adams, Julianne Bartlett, Matt Bell, Chris Candice, James Goodman, Susan LaBrier, Jamie Nelson, Andrew Pryor, Dylan Smith, Jeannita Triggs, Jaime R. Wood, Juliette Yancey

STAFF
Capuchina Taylor

EDITORIAL BOARD
John Dalton, Jennifer MacKenzie, Steven Schreiner, Howard Schwartz, Nanora Sweet, Mary Troy, Eamonn Wall

ADVISORY BOARD
Jeff Friedman, Ross Gay, Ruth Ellen Kocher, C. M. Mayo, Katherine Min, Naomi Shihab Nye, Tyrone Williams

Artwork, Eileen Ewen, "Lilacs"
Printed with permission of the artist and the University of Missouri–St. Louis.

Cover design by FOCUS/Graphics; page design by Adams Creative Services

Natural Bridge (ISSN 1525-9897) is published twice yearly by the Department of English, University of Missouri–St. Louis. The editors invite submissions of poetry, fiction, creative nonfiction, and translations during two periods each year: July 1–August 31 and November 1–December 31. Please address all correspondence to *Natural Bridge*, Department of English, University of Missouri–St. Louis, One University Blvd., St. Louis, Missouri 63121. Include a self-addressed, stamped envelope. Guidelines at www.umsl.edu/~natural. We do not accept electronic submissions.

Subscription rates in the United States for individuals are $15 for one year and $25 for two years; foreign rates for individuals are, respectively, $20 and $30. Subscription rates for institutions are $18 for one year and $30 for two years; foreign rates for institutions are, respectively, $23 and $35. Single issues are $8 (please include $3 for single-copy international orders). See our insert for a subscription form.

Natural Bridge is distributed by Ubiquity and is a member of the Council of Literary Magazines and Presses. It is indexed by *The Index of American Periodical Verse* and *The American Humanities Index*.

The publication of *Natural Bridge* is made possible by support from the Department of English of the University of Missouri–St. Louis and by a grant from the St. Louis Regional Arts Commission.

PRINT IN U.S.A. ON RECYCLED, ACID-FREE PAPER

CONTENTS

From the Guest-Editor v   Mary Troy

Fiction

Valerie Vogrin   1   Aim
Stephanie Dickinson   17   The Sweetness of Iraq
Kim Foster   35   Lifestyle
Claire Ibarra   55   A Glimpse of Color
Nathan Leslie   61   Just in Case
Ryan Stone   75   Catching Earl
Boris Vian   87   The Priest in Swim Trunks
                                 Translated by Julia Older
Aimee Loiselle   91   The Things You Take, the Things
                                 You Leave
Eric Paul Shaffer   111   Teacher of Athletes
John Michael Cummings   131   Bill the Lottery God
Charles R. Gillespie   148   A Rest for the Weary
Deb Jurmu   160   Breath of the Wok

Poetry

Mark D. Bennion   15   Sowing
Jürgen Becker   33   Correspondent
                                 Translated by Okla Elliott
Jessica M. Brophy   34   his back
Jan Pettit   52   I need to break laws
                                 Everything must go
Karen Hildebrand   54   Sleep Apnea
Claire Zoghb   60   The Relativity of Distance
Teri Ellen Cross   74   Wrath
Bridget Meeds   90   The Salmon of Knowledge
Carrie Shipers   108   Discards

Yu Xiang 109 2002, I Have
  Translated by Joanna Sit and Keming Liu

Zach Savich 129 Animal
David Dodd Lee 144 Calendar Series I: Wolf Spider
  Calendar Series I: Romantic
  Calendar Series I: Porcelain
  Calendar Series I: The Pyramids
Luisa A. Igloria 157 Journey To The West
  The Minim
Angela Vogel 178 Migraineur
Jason Lee Brown 180 Why Mr. President Loves Soap
  Bubbles

181 Contributors' Notes

From the Guest-Editor

Art alleviates boredom, and it does so by taking us out of ourselves and throwing us into the unfamiliar and the new, yet in the best works, that unfamiliar can turn back on itself and become recognizable as part of us, maybe that part we've deliberately pushed aside, or one briefly unrecognizable because seen from a different angle. Writers have always striven to "tell it slant," as Emily instructed, and as readers we remain delighted to read it slant.

How much is the slant? Well that depends on the talent and taste of the writer.

In this issue of *Natural Bridge*, the slant comes from a political campaign for justice of the peace in which the candidate runs on a promise to be crooked, from a woman who experimented with the swinging lifestyle, from an obsessed day trader who cannot stop gambling, from a young professional woman who chooses homelessness, from a veteran of the Iraq war, from a displaced Chinese man whose identity is not important to those who love him. It comes in the form of love poems and poems of the sacred and poems of war. It comes from a translated poem in which an identity is created from a list, and from a poem about intense combustible anger. It comes from a story written as a fable and a modular story written around but not about an event. It comes from the comic mixed with sorrow. The slant version of the truth can make you laugh or cry or both, can worry, irritate, annoy, or offend you, as well as move or delight you. That is the hope of all of us who worked on this issue.

From the more than one thousand submissions for this issue, all over the transom, not one piece solicited, we have accepted these 11 stories, 18 poems, and 3 translations. It goes without saying that we returned some good pieces, for we are human, and I, along with the editorial assistants, those MFA students who are advanced enough to serve as readers and editors, selected the pieces fast, but with as much care as possible. There was surprising unanimity on these, and we believe that each piece chosen for issue 19 is well-crafted and true and not boring.

The editorial assistants who worked so hard on this issue are Steven Adams, Olivia Ayes, Julianne Bartlett, Matt Bell, Chris Candice, James Goodman, Susan LaBrier, Jamie Nelson, Andrew Pryor, Dylan Smith, Jeannita Triggs, Jaime R. Wood, and Juliette Yancey. May their own work be considered with as much intelligence and care when they submit it to other journals.

—*Mary Troy*

Valerie Vogrin

AIM

P<small>ARR</small>

Occasionally, over the past couple of years, Parr dreamed about his sister, a recurring dream, identical each time in its particulars. The sun was just overhead, the white car eye-blinkingly bright, its right front tire running over the curb as she turned off Natural Bridge Road onto Hanley and down the hill toward his house. The dreams felt chemical, like freshly developed photographs, and he took them to have meaning. Several times, with different women, he'd said it aloud. "I feel it. She's coming back."

So far he'd been wrong. Premonition-wise, in that Margo had not come back or been found. And telling the women hadn't turned out right either. He told them because it was an interesting thing about himself, maybe, and he tended to run out of things to say. For a week or two's worth of dates he could talk about teaching English in Japan, living there for five years, and his month-long trip to Australia right before he moved back. But his part-time job at the preschool vaguely embarrassed him, as did the B's and C's he'd been earning in his night classes. The women, nice women, felt bad for him, but he wondered if he appeared pathetic, trotting out this tale of woe. Sympathy, he was coming to understand, wasn't an emotion that readily blossomed into love. Summers, his built-in swimming pool made him feel good about his prospects; in the cooler months he floundered.

He'd finished painting his bedroom the day before. Two-plus coats of a deep teal blue. The color didn't look quite right to him—more like a shade you'd expect to see on a boat. April had chosen it. When she first visited his house she remarked, "You need some color around here," a rare, and thus valuable, definitive statement. Parr hadn't acted on it right away. He waited until they'd been going out for a couple of months before he choreographed the trip to Home Depot for a drill bit, the detour through the paint department. Between the hefty student loan debt she'd amassed at Wash U and her modest salary as a public radio producer, she was as cash poor as Parr. Just last week she presented him a new shower curtain patterned with small black and white checks that wiggled when you stared at them. "Found it on the bus," she said, and he was nearly certain she was joking. If April agreed to move in he would promise to accelerate the renovations, paint every room in the house.

Still, Parr didn't want April to think he didn't have a mind of his own, so he bought new sheets and a comforter. White sheets because white was hopeful, and a dark gold comforter stitched with metallic gold thread. He was proud of this bold choice, though not at all confident. His dresser and nightstand looked shabby next to the new paint and bedding, but no one could say the room wasn't transformed.

"Very nice." He could hear that she meant it. Because she'd chosen semi-gloss, the paint still looked wet and Parr held his arms tight to his body. A silence fell on them, stuck in the threshold, looking at the bedroom like an exhibit in a museum. In moments like these he said things he shouldn't say. In a moment like this one he had told her about the dreams. This moment was rescued by a growl from her stomach.

"Hungry?" he asked.

Margo, Parr's missing sister, had last been seen eight years ago backing out of their mother's driveway in their mother's white Volvo, not with Shane, but with him still in the picture. If not for that, the whole scenario would have been a lot more optimistic to any mind, including Special Agent Fried's. Shane with the assault and manslaughter raps. Special Agent Fried with his nervous tugging at the tips of his walrus moustache.

Margo drove off, she'd drive back. That was the simple logic of his dream. The dream relinquished no clues regarding where she'd been and what she'd done. After her disappearance, Parr and his sisters, Angie and Twyla, had spent a ridiculous number of hours sitting around drinking red wine and smoking and imagining Margo's life.

One of the reasons he'd gone to Japan to begin with was to escape those pointless debates as to whether it was more likely that they'd headed for the east coast or the west coast or the Canadian or Mexican border. More people disappeared without a trace than you'd guess, Special Agent Fried said, but Parr had to think that they were the smart, methodical ones, not thugs like Shane or space cases like his sister.

Growing up, Parr was the only one in his family who really enjoyed playing board games and Margo was the only one who humored him, even after she moved out. She'd stop by once a week or so, after he'd gotten home from school, and they'd play checkers, although it was hard for her to sit still and she quite often forgot it was her turn in the middle of trying to figure out her next move. She regularly forgot the name of her bank, the name of her doctor, why she was crying. The last time he'd seen her she was wearing a wrinkled yellow cardigan, misbuttoned.

What Parr didn't tell anyone was that he'd come back from Japan and bought this house on Hanley because of the dream. Maybe the trick to premonitions was creating the conditions for them to be realized.

April didn't seem to mind that he stared at her. She was so beautiful to him that he focused on her in parts, so as to not be overwhelmed. As she chewed, for example, he studied her impossibly dainty nose. All other noses were blunt snouts compared to this one. Three freckles fell in a row, diagonally, across the bridge. Fitting, he thought—an ellipsis for a woman who left so much out. He'd never met anyone who spoke so little of herself.

"I like the way you cook vegetables," April said. "You've got el dente down pat."

At moments like this, Parr was almost positive she really did like him. "Have you given any more thought to Easter?"

"What are they like?"

"My family?" He didn't know how you could answer this question.

"Do they behave? Shout? Throw things?" April punctuated with her fork and a snow pea fell to the floor. She bent over to retrieve it, and when she was back to sitting upright Parr noted she was sneering slightly.

"No, no, nothing like that. Mom and Twyla sometimes get a little tipsy. Peabody, Angie's second husband, drinks, but quietly."

"Holidays are volatile in my experience."

"My niece, Polly, is seven. You can always play with her. I mean, that's what I do if things start getting heavy," he said. "Not that things generally get heavy. Mom can be kind of critical and Mom's husband, Nick, sneaks into the kitchen and eats things he's not supposed to eat because of his diabetes. That's about it."

"I don't know. What about Margo?"

"Don't worry," he said, "it almost never comes up." Parr left it at that.

ANGIE

As her dreams go, it's a positive one. She's with Parr in Japan, playing pinball in an enormous arcade. There's a crowd gathered around them because she's got some kind of magic touch going with the flippers and a hip-bounce, and the pinball machine is going crazy, emitting sound bites of cheering and applause and a few measures of martial-sounding music on top of the arrhythmic ringing and clanging that accompanies the accumulation of points. Her feet ache. The arcade's floor is concrete and she's been playing for hours. She's always tired in her dreams. Angie hadn't visited Parr in Japan. She had told him she was coming, that she'd bought a ticket, even. And then she told him that Polly had the mumps and she couldn't come after all. She didn't know how she felt about that—his unquestioning acceptance of her flimsy story. But she was so relieved when he moved back. They didn't feel like a family with him gone.

What she'd never told anyone was that a week before her disappearance she'd given Margo money—three hundred dollars—after they'd all sworn not to do that anymore.

The dryer had gone out the previous weekend. It had tumbled the cold wet clothes for several hours before she'd gotten suspicious. Since Peabody had started drinking again things like that tended to get past her. Pop Tarts she'd thought well-hidden, eaten by her thirteen-year-old son, Henry, whom she'd found more than once in the pantry, long past midnight, shoveling tablespoonfuls of sugar from the five-pound bag into his mouth. The cat bowl empty for some number of days and the cat not returned, a fact she hoped to keep from Polly. Now it was Easter, and yesterday, before she and Polly had dyed the eggs, she'd washed all the curtains in the house, re-hung them wet, and opened the windows, which she hoped would make them dry faster, and she kept the windows open overnight, because it seemed like clean, dry curtains might make up for her inadequacies as a homemaker and hostess. She was the only one with a table large enough to seat all the adults.

"Angie, you're a damn fool," Peabody said. The furnace had never been quite up to the task of warming their drafty bungalow. He paced the length of the house and looked thirsty for Jameson's.

"Once the oven gets going, it'll warm up in here." But she'd forgotten that her mother was bringing the ham and Twyla was bringing pies and supposedly Parr and his newish girlfriend were bringing a hot side dish, so she didn't really need to turn on the oven. She pushed the thermostat up another couple of notches and decided to bake cookies and leave the windows as they were.

There wasn't money for a new dryer or the power bill, but that was business for another day. It was going to be hard to maintain a festive attitude if she got started on the list of things they didn't have money for.

"I'm thankful for you, Miss Polly-wolly-pudding-all-day," she told her daughter. Peabody's thinking-about-drinking made Polly nervous, too, but now that Angie had her busy stirring the cookie batter, she was humming, despite her stated skepticism regarding the concept of Easter cookies.

"Hearts?" She snorted when Angie pulled the cookie cutter from the drawer.

"It's hearts or Christmas trees."

Polly's hair was pulled into sloppy braids. The hanks were uneven and the part ambled crookedly down the back of her head, but fixing them would disturb the moment. The whiskey bottle was in the cupboard behind where Polly sat on the stool at the countertop and Peabody wouldn't ask her to move, not so early in the day anyway. They made the icing while the cookies baked. Polly added tiny drops of color, one at a time, to three small bowls, creating perfect pale shades of yellow, pink, and blue.

So things were going fairly well until Twyla called to say that their mother and Nick wouldn't be coming. Nick was having a tingling in his toes and fingers. Twyla would pick up the ham on the way over. "A tingling?"

"Don't start, Ange. Be relieved. Everybody will have a better time with Mom not there."

Angie considered the curtains. She hoped she hadn't gone through all that rigmarole just for her mother. "She could have called earlier."

"She says they kept hoping the tingling would stop."

"Tingling!" Angie knew that in being petulant she was answering her own question, why their mother hadn't called her directly. "Okay. Whatever. Why don't you come over a little early, hang out before Parr gets here?"

"Is he still bringing the girl?"

"As far as I know."

This April person was either cold or avoiding Parr or both, holing up in the kitchen. She hadn't so much as dipped a finger into the buttery icing.

"Peabody won't say what he thinks." Angie slapped icing onto the too-warm cookies.

"Did he know Margo?"

"No, he and I met later that year."

"Maybe he thinks you won't like what he has to say."

"As if that's ever stopped him." Angie wasn't really thinking about what she was saying. *Did* she care what Peabody did or didn't say? "I think she's dead." Angie shook her head angrily. She was spattering icing all over the place. She had never spoken these words. Was this what she really believed or was it what she hoped? It would be a disaster, wouldn't it, if Margo returned now? With Margo gone it didn't matter that Angie hadn't liked her for a long time, that Margo had hurt them all, betrayed them in countless petty ways. But what was she doing talking about this anyway? It had been years, really, since it had been the big hot topic, and she and Twyla and their mother had made this official before Parr moved home—no more Margo talk. Parr was the youngest and he had loved Margo in a better, uncomplicated way. None of them wanted to send him back to that loss. Yet now, something about this girlfriend of his was goading her on.

"Margo had a quality that men couldn't resist—a vagueness they hoped to bring into focus. She had the skinniest wrists and she wore twenty bangles at a time, which meant she had to keep her arms cocked or they'd drop right off. That's how I remember her—left hand on her left shoulder, gazing out the window at something that wasn't there." This April was a cool customer, sitting with her hands folded in her lap, all ears.

"She was always like that, long before she started drinking and doing drugs. She didn't belong here, she told me that once. And that's how she lived her life—like she was just waiting for someone to realize that a mistake had been made and get her the hell out of here."

Peabody had snuck up on her. He rested his hands on her shoulders. "Does anybody really feel like they *belong* here? I mean, what would that mean exactly—to feel at home in the land of greed and plenty?"

"I do, *I* belong here." Angie jumped up from her chair. "Don't try to make me feel bad about that. I'm supposed to be here, with you and Polly and Henry."

"We were talking about Margo," April said.

Angie whipped around to face her. Tattletale! *Now* she spoke.

"This is why I drink," Peabody said, pouring a juice glass full of whiskey.

"Why is that?" April asked.

"Helps the medicine go down."

"Drinking makes things easier for you?"

Angie didn't understand the question. What other reason was there?

"More or less," Peabody said.

"What's going on in here?" Parr stood in the threshold. His face was pinched with concern. "Twyla wants to know when we're going to eat."

"I'm getting to know your family, Parr."

Oh, she was a peach all right.

Peabody chimed in. "Angie here thought it'd be a good day to talk about Margo."

Poor Parr, he seemed to shrink in the doorway. He looked at Angie expectantly.

She nodded. "It's true. It's not healthy to not talk about it."

"Christ, Angie. It's history." Peabody refilled his juice glass.

"You're a lizard. You don't have feelings. *You* don't belong here. What are you doing here anyway?" Angie grabbed his glass and gulped down the whiskey. She might as well be speaking in tongues. The whiskey burnt her mouth and throat.

Peabody snatched the bottle and shoved past Parr.

"Are you okay?" Parr asked.

They left her alone in the kitchen to cool off. But she wasn't upset, exactly. Her body was possessed by a strange relief. She was lightheaded, buoyant—as if her pores were expiring tiny plumes of helium. It would be frightening to feel this free all the time.

She frosted two sheets of cookies, taking enough time that they would think she was penitent. When she heard The Cars playing she knew Peabody had found something else to drink. There it was, an empty liter of red wine on the coffee table, another one started, and full glasses all around. Twyla and Peabody leaned back groggily on the couch. They must have started before Peabody had come in for the whiskey. Twyla had kicked off her insanely pink patent leather sling-backs and her pink linen shift was scrunched at her waist. The platters of cookies she'd sent in—leaving herself alone with April to begin with—had been devoured. Parr was playing Parcheesi with Henry. Henry's mouth was smeared with pink icing and Parr's was smeared with yellow. The cuffs on Henry's shirtsleeves hit a full inch above his wrist bones. The room was just plain cold. She slammed shut the windows in the living room and the dining room, saw that someone had set the table.

Tucked into the alcove, in the chair beside the bricked up fireplace, April sat, brushing out Polly's braids. The thick brown waves bristled with static electricity. April's glass looked like whiskey. She held two green elastic bands between her lips. Angie felt a tickle of irritation. Parr must have been watching her, seen it on her face. He leapt to his feet, nearly knocking over his glass of wine, and swept Polly out of April's reach.

"Where have you hidden your chocolate bunnies, little girl?" Parr held her at the waist, upside down, the tips of her hair brushing the floor. He swung her from side to side like a human broom.

Polly squealed and giggled. "I'm not going to tell you."

Now Henry got into it, came over and started tickling Polly's sides, and she squealed louder.

"Save me," she cried. "Save me!" She flung her head around, looking for a rescuer.

Henry kept at it. "There's no hope for you. Buwhahaha!"

Polly started kicking. Parr ducked his head and held her out a bit further from his body. Was she still having fun? Her voice sounded a little frantic. "Oh, somebody, please help me!"

APRIL

Their damn sister was just gone. As gone as the fifth chair flute player you sat next to for three years in high school, never finding it necessary to challenge her, because how was fifth chair in any substantive way better than sixth? And then you graduate and never hear from her again. There were hundreds of people like that in a person's life, right? All the folks you worked beside for a couple of months or years in disposable jobs. You knew the names of their kids and their parents' ailments and how many pounds they hoped to lose before swimsuit season. Neighbors, landlords, and the UPS guy when you were buying a lot of stuff online. The people in the coffee shops and video stores and public libraries who were a regular presence in your life until you moved to another state and threw away the membership cards and library cards and so forth. You could fill a stadium, probably, with all those people. People who were just gone, as you were just gone to them.

It was the first day of pool season, April 24th, 85 degrees, humid. It had taken the better part of the last thirty-six hours to fill the pool with very cold water. Parr had swum laps before he went to buy meat and buns and stuff for a cookout. He had that walrusy layer of fat on him. He slept naked year round, apparently. Even in January and February when he woke in the middle of the night and couldn't get back to sleep, he just pulled on boxers and sat on the couch drinking green tea and watching snippets of movies on cable. She figured that if she was a nice person she would have gotten up to keep him company, at least once, but instead she rolled over onto his side of the bed, enveloped in his leftover warmth.

Peabody lounged on an inflatable red raft in the middle of the pool with a can of Budweiser balanced on his stomach. He drifted like a leaf, vaguely clockwise.

Just before Parr left for the store he brought April a stack of old *Time* magazines and a bowl of red delicious apples. He opened his mouth and closed it. Opened it again. Put his big palm over her left knee. "I can't believe you're here," he said.

"Look at this zit on my chin," she said. "Do illusions have zits like this?" She willed him to let it rest. She glanced over at Peabody.

"I mean, that you're *still* here."

"Parr!"

"What? I was so lonely and I hoped more than anything that I would meet someone smart and wonderful like you."

She wanted to tell him that these were things you shouldn't tell another person. But he would ask why and it would be impossible to explain.

Just after Parr left she went inside for a soda. The kitchen smelled like sawdust and the grit felt weirdly good beneath her bare feet. Peabody appeared beside her, covered with goosebumps.

"You're dripping," she said. What kind of person didn't even grab a towel? Parr had set out a stack of freshly laundered beach towels on a Rubbermaid table right next to the pool.

"I wondered what you were up to." Peabody bee-lined for the cupboard where Parr kept the grocery bags. He did a double-take, apparently confounded by the missing cupboard doors. Kneeling, he rummaged behind the sacks and pulled a dusty bottle of Bushmills from the back. He wiped it off on his sopping swim trunks. "So what's with you and Parr?" he asked. "You got some kind of beauty and the beast vibe going?"

"Go away, Peabody. You don't amuse me."

"I'm not trying to amuse you."

"You have the soul of an old potato."

"Just your type, huh?"

Exactly.

She'd had no business even meeting Parr. She'd left the after-work gathering at the over-priced vodka bar, feeling smudged by the banality of the conversation—petty mumblings over promotions and fundraising skullduggery. A full, margarine-yellow moon hung lazily in the sky and she took it as a sign to stop for a drink. She liked drinking alone at unfamiliar bars, bumming smokes from strangers. There were three bars more or less in a row on Kingshighway, just south of Chippewa. She could walk home if she had to. She chose the bar in the middle, the one she was sure she'd never been in before. Parr had driven across town only because Twyla's goddaughter had just gotten a job bartending there. A job she held onto for only a couple of weeks.

When April walked in, Parr was singing karaoke, a slightly flat rendition of "I Fall to Pieces." She almost walked out then, but she already had the bartender's eye.

"How'd I do?" he asked. His forehead was sweaty. "I'm not sure that song was my best choice." Turned out she'd taken the seat right next to the one he'd claimed. How had she missed the bottle of Bud sitting there? Parr was so not-smooth, so goofy. At the end of the night, when he insisted on walking her out to her car, she still didn't want anything to do with him, yet she'd told him all about her job, her money worries. She'd liked Parr's stories about living in Japan. It was comical, the picture of this big, galumphing guy shambling through the crowds of compact, orderly people.

Before she could escape inside her car, Parr pulled her to him in a hot, awkward bear hug. "I'd go home with you right now," he told her between kisses, as if that was even on the table.

Recently, Parr had asked her how many lovers she'd had. He imagined, perhaps, that their combined number—his and hers—would fit neatly on two hands or create some other romantic configuration that would confirm that they were *meant to be together*.

She cut her best guess in half and halved it again, and then once more for good measure. Twelve, she said, and took care to attach a period to her answer. The look on his face, a tense flattening of his chin and cheeks, made her wish she'd told him the truth, that she didn't know, couldn't remember them all, probably had forgotten as many as she remembered. "Does it matter?" she asked him, daring him to say yes. Then she chickened out, grabbed his cock before he could answer.

"Too bad I'm a happily married man, huh?" Peabody pressed his erection against her hip.

She shuddered. "Bloody shame."

If there was somebody for everybody, maybe the trick was to avoid your somebody. Maybe ending up with a person who was all wrong for you was the best possible outcome. She took a deep breath. She'd need her strength to deal with the rest of the clan.

His family! Neither sister had liked her. What would the mother be like, for God's sake? As they shook hands Twyla's sharply tweezed eyebrows undulated and her nostrils flared. April could tell they'd been hopeful, that they really did want someone for their brother, and they were put out that she wasn't what they had in mind. April thought she had erased herself into nondescriptness—no makeup, no perfume, and the blandest outfit she could come up with, pressed khakis and a navy blue cable knit sweater. What had Twyla seen? Smelled? The same thing Peabody was sniffing after?

In her dream the woman looked a lot like Gwyneth Paltrow, only April knew it was Margo. (Gwyneth after a month-long bender in Reno, Gwyneth with stomach trouble and chronic headaches and a bad haircut.) Margo was sitting at Parr's dining room table making bead bracelets with Polly and April. Almost as many beads got dropped onto the god-awful shag carpet as got strung onto the elastic thread. Tiny plastic primary colored beads that would be ground into the two-toned green fibers and never be vacuumed up.

Peabody was arranged like a target: the aquamarine oval of the pool, the red rectangular raft, the sunburnt man, a shiny aluminum can. He lifted his head and winked at her. Bastard. It pissed her off how drinking eased things for him. Drinking only dulled her, made her feel like she was wrapped in cotton in a snap-shut jewelry box. He'd pay for it, she figured, but look at him now! Not a care in the world. She grabbed an apple. Wound up. Aimed for the can on his belly.

PARR

Parr could tell that April really liked the pool. She'd brought over two bikinis and two kinds of sunblock. He thanked the weather gods for summer's early onset. He didn't feel good about leaving her alone with Peabody, who had shown up at noon sharp in his swim trunks as if he'd received an engraved invitation. That was when Parr got the idea for a barbeque. A crowd would be better. Get Henry and Polly and some of their friends over—that was the ticket. April would see that his family really could have fun. Peabody was an agent of unease. And Easter had been such a disaster.

"Well that was fun!" April had thrown her big straw purse on the couch. Her keys clanged inside it. He didn't turn on the lamp, but she snapped on the overhead light in the kitchen. He sat beside her purse as she banged around in the cupboards—a glass and the aspirin bottle pulled out. The water ran and ran. He shoved the purse out of sight beneath the couch. He waited for her to reappear. Lit from behind, she seemed to be vibrating. He thought she might hurl the water glass at him.

"I'm so sorry," he said. "I had no idea—"

She turned her back on him. "Forget it. Let's fuck."

He didn't know what else to do. She was already naked when he got to the bedroom. He imagined that April was on fire and he hurled himself against her like a blanket to stifle the flames.

Even afterward, he was afraid she might say something more, something he wouldn't want to hear. He slid to the end of the bed and rubbed her feet, worked his thumbs into her arches until she moaned. He nibbled at her right ankle. Ran his tongue up the ridge of her shin. Kissed a tiny, white crescent-shaped scar on her knee. Why did everything have to be so unsettled? He made his mind a blank screen. What did he really think had happened to Margo? April's knee tasted flat, like bare wood. He couldn't make the blankness take shape. This was a new kind of blankness, with no image attached to it at all, not even a shape or a color or hiss of static. And no car rounding the corner. No car. No road. No rotting body, no mildewed efficiency apartment in a distant city, no hotel room, no jail cell—as though Margo had traveled further away when he wasn't paying attention. No longer missing, but truly disappeared. He began to weep.

"I'm sorry, Parr." April pushed herself to sitting. "We all drank too much. It doesn't mean anything. Okay?" She wiped his tears with her fingertips. Such a tender gesture. He was afraid to look at her face, in case her expression didn't match. He pressed his lips to her knee. Again, he emptied his mind. Eyes closed, eyes open, it didn't matter. He could see only what was in front of him. Skin. That scar, like one half of a parentheses. The briefest bit of punctuation.

Mark D. Bennion

SOWING

We dropped it all. Beyond the drafts of reed
and mangrove, backs strapped to makeshift
plow-shares propelling their harrows deep

into the black soil. Palms juggled scurf
of fig pip and chick peas, scratches of *hitta*
and barley. Fingers sold-out to the sliver

of quince, tossing down *tappuach* in the form
of blood-drops or the wooden pit of apricots.
The elders aligned to need.

Several mothers girded each pruning hook
then tamed horse and ass, encircled cows,
yammered tunes to the wild goats.

How each of us wore the yoke of the ox
and the acrid slip of its feculent dung.
There was myrtle and ochre in this passage,

rows of *summaq* and its barbs of fruit.
From land to land we sidled every last
spice, furrowed benediction out of clove

and chicle, caressed the green tips of wild leeks
as mud dried on our tired fingers. Not everyone
stomached the native lentils, *orez*, and vetch,

but we knew we were home in the abundance
of laurels, the cool bob of ferns. This exchange
of tutor and style freed us from the infinite desert

and the children teased as their fathers
explained the mystery of bulbs and mushrooms;
even the infants greened in the *yoreh*.

It's not enough to say our heads haloed
in this swabbing gestation, especially
when we rendered to our budding sons

and daughters the boll and tuber, kernel and pod.
They foresaw the foxtail and crocus, the heady
orange blossom and strident blue squill.

Indeed, they were already black mustards
stirring the field or the symmetry of sorrels
in their want of rain after the heat of the sun.

Stephanie Dickinson

THE SWEETNESS OF IRAQ

Even under the shade of my headgear it's at least five degrees hotter inside the vehicle. The sky is a gray powder like the houses and mud they're made of. My eyes crave leaves, grass and trees, anything green to lick the moisture from. Staff Sergeant Tonto and Specialist Boyd ride up front. Our translator Amman rides in back of the Humvee with me and Goliath, the ordnance disposal robot. "Specialist Bethany," he says, "you think Goliath is your pet." I find myself touching the 'bot, its sensors and grasshopper legs. When I'm in my bomb suit, Goliath is my man. And this is the land of the goddess of chaos—Tiamat who created demons from animal and human parts. We're part of a convoy heading into the country of the mounds. The Tigris and Euphrates from whence came the clay for the first cuneiform writing. Amman tells of the Iraq cavefish, how they are colorless and blind from living underground. Their heads and lips and barbells are flecked with taste buds. They taste their environment. "In still waters they flick their tail slowly. When obstacles are met," he says, "the fish simply turns gently away at the last possible minute."

The road shimmers before me; the trees cocooned with ice lick and kiss the headlights. I'm taking the long roundabout way from the farm into town. I can't put off any longer looking for Moses. The pickup seems to know where it's going down the deserted road that stands out clear between the banks of snow. My wipers are icing over and I stop and open the window and reach out with the long handled ice scraper and give the wiper a whack. I take the curve by the power plant, its blinking red lights lonely in the snow. The pickup swerves. My right hand grabs back the wheel. I substitute my knee for my left hand.

More gravel ice is pinging against the headlights and I'm hot like I swallowed Red Bull and cayenne. Straight ahead in the road a piece of rubber tire sits and I jam on the brakes. My heart races as I ease the door to the pickup open and slide out. I move toward the ditch where branches broken from the overhang of hardwoods jut. Their still clinging snow leaves are frozen. Milk nipples. I pull the branch free and turn, scouring the periphery of ditches. This is the long slow walk in the shadow of a trip wire. Something skitters from the brush. Dog, rabbit, wild pig. Native ghosts. I whirl, the crust of snow is blank, no phantoms of prairie grass. I listen for the muffled hoot of a snow owl.

Idiot, get the job finished, you're good at this. I prod the rubber for a timing device. The left side of my face itches, each pore seeps its own fear stink. Work the stick, do it easy, now lift it. Boom, you're dead. I stay in my crouch. Nothing. The piece of rubber tire is plain rubber. I look up. The moon waxes full, the face of a pale blue Persian cat floating in the sky. Her litter torn from her womb and scattered into bits of fur and gore to make the stars.

Maybe I'm calling the snow when I sit in the truck with the engine off in the parking lot of the Tender Trap, slugging back my bottle of Demerol. The flakes are falling like strings of a gauzy shawl. Lillian's bound to be bartending and she may know where Moses is. Liquid Demerol and I make a pretty couple giving me a good reason to go into that tavern and show myself. Blizzard, the owner, used to serve my underage butt when I was with Lillian, all the while making goo-goo eyes at her. Moses, he'd card and kick out. I'm twenty-two and legal now. I click the interior light and grab the rearview mirror and twist it vertical. The scar runs like rickrack from the corner of my mouth over the dent in my jaw where the bone is gone. I untube my lip gloss and smear it on. I spit. There's six-year old Bethany running down the farm lane, ice under the new snow catching and tripping her. "Mom, the snow hurt me. Do you love me, Mom?" Boom, you're dead.

I take three steps toward the back entrance of the Tender Trap, an old slaughterhouse beer tavern. Across the vacant lot is where Lillian and Moses lived in a trailer after their parents split and their mom moved them into town. Nothing remains, not the propane tank and front steps, not their inebriated mom tiptoeing between the snow-drifts in her bare feet, her sad brown eyes laughing. *Catch me, if you can.*

The sheik invites us into his house where we sit on the floor to enjoy his hospitality. First are kebobs, hunks of musky grilled goat, then thick red lentil soup. No one uses a spoon. "I'm not going to eat that. Haji wipe their shit with their left hand. I've never seen toilet paper in this country," Specialist Boyd says, his mouth fat with Haji kebob. I make myself chew, my mouth tastes like dust. Two days ago we evacuated a nearby village so we could safely explode a device. A little girl was hiding in a food cupboard and the explosion took part of her face. The girl is the sheik's niece. The sheik's house holds the heat of the desert. Amman is speaking in dark Arabic sentences, like loops of molasses, a rich stickiness hangs from his chin. More food. The next course is pacha, a dish made of sheep, all of the animal, the stomach, the feet, the kidneys, and brains, nothing wasted. The sheik turns to me. "You are the bomb demolisher." On his fingers is the pale oily eye of a sheep. "You are the one who altered the face of my sister's child."

There are garbage cans on the back step and scruffy weeds poke up in the snow. I stomp my boots on the top step and make myself walk inside over the black and red linoleum. The hallway turns into a bar room with a pool table, a foos ball game, and the last jukebox in Cedar Rapids, Iowa. The Pabst Blue Ribbon beer clock gives off a blue glow. Older guys shoot pool and women in flannel shirts sit at tables drinking pitchers of beer. It could have been yesterday, not years ago.

"Hey, chickie," I say, approaching her.

The bartender, Lillian, leans against the till. "What do you want, partner?" The light is bad but I take her in, her long dark hair and permanently tan skin. Lillian, looking like the Delta Lady, a native woman in Levis. Then she does a double-take. "BETHANY!" Damn it's Bethany." She rushes out from behind the bar in her tank top and pierced belly button and child-size turquoise high heels the middle of winter and throws her arms around me. Her hair smells of smoke and snow. "Let me get a look at you." When she steps back her eyes fill. My brunette hair is growing out thick from its bald fuzz and I've got it parted on my left side. Bits of shrapnel inside my eyelid make a purplish shadow. I leave my cape on that Mom made. I'm dressed in black and white, black jeans, black boots, a pressed white shirt with the left long sleeve pinned up over the residual of my elbow, which is Walter Reed speak for stump.

"Damn," she says letting out a low whistle. "So you blew yourself up." A laugh boils out of her throat. Her stare frightens me, then she holds my face between her hands and kisses me smack on the lips.

I have to laugh too. Lillian leads me to a stool and presses a napkin on the bar in front of me. "Take off that Zorro cape and stay awhile or are you planning on robbing us?" She touches my cheek and her fingertips feel cool. I wrap the cape around me, satin swirls around my hips. I'm taking in how much the same everything is, those abalone chip mobiles that tremble whenever the door opens. Packets of Sugar Rite and ketchup in silver pitchers, a crusty bottle of horseradish. I scratched my initials on the horseradish label before I deployed and sure enough the letters BT are still there.

"Nobody's used that horseradish in twenty two months. I've been around the world and that bottle hasn't moved."

"Trust me, it's moved. Blizzard likes it nice and clean in here. His wife finally passed away and he wants to make it legal." Lillian struts over to the pickled egg jar, lifts the lid and sticks her hand into the eggs that look like eyeballs bobbing in vinegar. She holds it out to me and hooks one of her spike heels over the rung of the stool." Here have an egg. You still love them?"

"Yup."

"Where you living? On the farm with Mom?"

"Yup." I take a bite of sour egg. "Come spring I'm planting an orchard."

Lillian jangles her armload of bracelets, gets up and goes behind the bar. She slits the cellophane on a cheeseburger and roast beef sandwich and sticks them in the microwave set for one minute and forty seconds. "What kind?"

"Apples, nectarines, peaches." I bow my head to the fire that sizzles through what is left of my left arm, the hand that is not there clenches.

I can see the orchard in my mind's eye left over from my great-grandmother's time. Planted in the days when diphtheria and smallpox traveled the roads. A few straggly apple trees but in spring festering with blossoms, lip-skin pink, every twig sweated in scent. Lillian and I would wade into the orchard, chin ourselves, swing legs up, and then rub blossoms on our neck, wrists, and beginning breasts.

Lillian buys me a draft. I sip the foam off a dark beer and then turn to check out the guy at the end of the bar. He's staring. I take another mouthful of sour beer. "Yup, that's who you think it is." She sets a tequila shooter in front of me, a saucer of cut lemons and a salt shaker. How's that going to mix with my Demerol? The stuff I have to take to sit up straight. "Moses bought this for you, chickie." She lifts an eyebrow that she's blackened in. "My twin brother got out of Anamosa a year ago. He's still on parole. I won't serve him anything but soda and water."

Moses, Lillian, and Bethany. The outcast trinity. Moses dropped out of high school the year their father was arrested for public lewdness, and then the son started getting in trouble. You never saw the sheriff's vehicle on Jappa Road until Moses held up Bob's Polka Barrel Tavern. The sheriff claimed he took the whole damn cash register.

"Bethany?" the guy at the end of the bar says.

A foos ball player kicks a goalie, a spin around the metal pole.

"Moses," I answer. I don't intend to say anything stupid like 'How are you?'

He's wearing a sheepskin vest, his dark hair is cowlicky and tied into a pug tail, and a few shorter wisps hang down. His skin is clay and his eyes are the dusty black skins of concord grapes with long sticky eyelashes. I don't need to see him up close to know that. He gets up off the stool and walks over. We shake and when I lift my fingers to my nose it's there—the odor of grape jelly. I've always known him, his face in the kindergarten class picture, and his twin sister next to him. We rode the same school bus. I pick up the tequila, pour it down and then bite into a lemon to cut the burn. It mixes with the pain meds. "How's your dad doing?" I ask, like I care and maybe I do. Their father was a wrinkled hired man who drank at Bob's Polka Barrel and once pissing on the street exposed himself to a child. Moses and I keep looking. Handsome, lean, his muscle is wound to bone like pipe threads. The bruises on his neck must be hickeys, the red and purple giant kind. I picture his girlfriend with soft lips and inch long fingernails dipped in stardust. "That's some suck mark." It comes out of my mouth without passing through my brain.

He chuckles, "Darling, that's a spider bite."

We've just got in and the sweat forms a paste over my chest. I pull on my fatigues in my sleeping bag; slip my knife into my pocket. The path to the latrines is far away and unlit. Heat rash is breaking out in nests over my butt cheeks. I scratch until my fingernails bleed. I grab my shaving kit and head to the showers. The moon shocks me shining down. Beautiful here too. Dust moon. Mud moon. Bald lens of a high vision goggle. The showers share a wall with the latrines. A female voice. "Don't." Then a male voice. "Just grind with me." I step under the falling water. The voices are falling too. They mix together with the paste on my body. "I hate penises. I hate the way you guys love it, stroke it," the female bursts. "Like your hand is silk, then wringing its neck." I plug my ears and stand under the water but I still hear. "Dyke!"

Moses orders a sandwich. Blood shimmers on the sliced raggedy beef. He dips his finger in it, and then licks. Since his release he's lived over at the Tin Lantern Motel, details cars, and does custom paint jobs, some hieroglyphics and gang tag vehicles. My eyes fix on the crease of his jeans. The cuff of his shirt, how it rides his forearm, the hairs there, and the last button stitched with red.

"Want to play some pool?" he asks, rubbing chalk on the end of a cue.

"I'd like to watch you play."

He orders me another shooter, but sticks to beer for himself. Moses plays, pocketing the balls. "Do you want to see where I live?" he asks, explaining The Lantern's not far and that he's on foot.

"Sure," I say, the red flush in my forehead. We first had sex when we were fourteen, and the last time we were nineteen. I'd just enlisted and wanted him to sign up too. The Army's hard up and letting in those who have morally lapsed. Moses had laughed.

I give Moses the keys to the pickup, ask him to drive, and then he opens the door for me and tucks the hem of my cape in before going around to the driver's side. I like the way he uses the stick shift, smooth glances over his shoulder. I remember how the ground breathed and whenever the furrows made fog we crawled to each other, pretending to be earthworms. After he robbed the tavern they kept him in jail while they searched his car, ripped up the floorboards and finding jack had to let him go. "Maybe that will slow you down," Lillian said, when she bailed him out. A week later he failed to stop for the highway patrol and they put on their cherry top lights. He just didn't feel like stopping and took off in an old Toyota down Waubek Road doing ninety-one miles per hour and there was Farmer Zach's pickup in the middle of the road with its hood up. Moses swerved for the ditch but the backend fishtailed and ran the old man over.

Cedar Rapids seems pretty much the same with a few low lying lights, K-Mart and Subway and the silos of the Quaker Oats Factory, Wilson's Meatpacking Plant and Little Bohemia, another tavern where the meatpackers drink the taste of blood from their throats. Then the 16th Avenue Bridge with its balustrade and broken lions, Cedar Rapids, whose sister city is Prague. Those crippled beasts mimic the older city's bridge.

Moses riffs on the conditions of life and how even here far from the market machine the devolution is happening. "Who says evolution operates in only one direction, Bet?"

Under the snow all the rich black soil is choking from chemicals and anyone who worked the fields is getting sick with lymphoma, including his old man, who drove tractor for Zach Farms and used to come home white from insecticide. They called him snowman. Everything the pioneer whites made from blackberry preserves to lavender talc, from church and chicken noodle soup suppers to scrub boards and anvils, has vanished. The work horses plowing, the sweating shoulder-high July corn, the patchwork quilt homesteads and fencing, the hay mounds and vegetable gardens, the windmills and cisterns, all finished. Gone. What's left? Factory animals, factory farms, control of the seeds. Everyone drugged. Everything gone to fast foods and pharmaceuticals. You call this a free country? You think you fought for freedom? Pretty soon you'll need a prescription to buy Vitamin C. There's darkness around the bend. The slaughtered wolves are angry. So is the blue grass. He's seen them in dreams, the headless chickens that search for their eyes, feathers trying to attach themselves. All the sacrifices gone to farm sales and sell outs, die-offs of wild geese, cloned cows with two heads giving milk, mad cow, mad dog. The native peoples will reappear when the market whites have killed the water, the air, the earth.

And then Moses laughs. "I'd like that to happen. A die-off of people so the animals left on this planet could survive."

"How would you cause a die-off to happen?"

"People restricted to a diet of Skittles and Diet Coke. That doesn't include you, Bet."

All bets are off. *Bet*, his nickname for me.

It's a man's room. When Moses opens the door the smell of grape jelly and incense rushes at me. The bed takes up most of the room with its bed board painted gold and there's a tapestry pinned to the wall. On the dresser a pile of books and CDs and pennies and dimes and on the little round table with the room's one chair are knives and squares of sandpaper and chunks of wood and birds and figurines, a wooden dagger. He's still whittling. Pretty things. He closes the door and pulls the chain lock. I sit on the bed. It needs fortification like the perimeter of a checkpoint. The green bedspread is beautiful as a willow grove, but the ceiling seems too low. My belly aches from the tequila. There's an alleyway up on the ceiling and a gray house and a boy riding his bicycle through brown liquid where the sewer has exploded. In the alley, piss and graffiti on the walls.

Moses sits next to me on the bed, he jiggles his legs like his foot is doing some thinking on its own and might want to run. I need

Demerol. "You want to talk about anything, Bethany? Like why you didn't contact me and my sister. I know we're bums but three months you've been back and not a word."

I shrug. I tell him I intend to be a one-armed orchard farmer, who raises apples and those peaches with blond flesh that are smaller and tougher than Georgia peaches. Peaches with a bite of winter in them.

He lays his hand over mine. I don't know if I ever want to be touched again. I move my hand.

His dark eyes widen. "You're among friends here, you know that, Bet."

Yeah, sure, easy to say.

I'm still in the shower. The voices from the latrine have quieted. One hundred and ten degrees and the brain functions differently. The synapses shatter, the cerebral cortex melts. The animal brain takes over, the lower instincts. Then I hear a buzzing. Like the proposed new generation bomb sniffers. Bees. The buzzing passes by. Like a village girl with half a cheek and no bottom teeth, like a bag of Doritos. I use a scraper on my feet, dig at the calluses. I hear someone come in the women's shower trailer. "It's in use," I call out, letting the lukewarm water spew over me. The door opens and there's the smell of pot. Sergeant Tonto and Specialist Boyd enter with towels over their arms. "Sir, this is against regulation." What's that? My eyes widen. Tonto puts the lit end of the joint into his mouth, he blows a gush of hot smoke into my mouth, it hits the back of my tonsils. There's another joint in Boyd's mouth. This joint is fat, a mealy weedy smell, like the fires of the Baghdad dump, miles of shit and garbage spontaneously combusting. "Get the fuck out of here, sir," I say to Tonto. His eyes change color. Yes, I once saw a lizard change from blue to pink to green back to blue. They do it by breathing air into their blood. The lizard's throat bloats out like a rooster's comb and becomes blood red. Then its cheeks puff out and he turns indigo blue. Tonto's eyes are blue then red then black. There's a bottle of mouthwash, they drink from. Gin shipped from the states blended with green food coloring.

Moses stands against the dresser, plugs in a coffee pot. An outlet with a thicket of cords.

"Give me your cape, woman, you're staying." Moses reaches to untie the bow at my neck that my mom tied earlier. I can hear her words trying to help. "It's more a dent in your face than anything and a dent isn't so bad. And hold your shoulders straight, even if it's a beer tavern you don't want to look crooked. Honestly, Bethany, why won't you wear that prosthesis? You can hardly tell the difference."

The satin and flannel slides off me and there I am in a white shirt with a pinned- up sleeve. I'm shivering fully dressed. I'm too naked. The mirror is right there staring. Moses kneels before me. He goes quiet and I'm watching those wisps of hair trailing over his ears, not too large like satellite dishes or tiny like dollhouse teacups, just right.

I jut my chin out, wait for him to say something, dare him. I clench my fist.

"You know I don't judge."

I'm remembering how once we played King of the Hill in the soybean bin, both of us nine years old and not knowing until it was too late that soybeans sifted, rolled against each other and sucked you in like quicksand. We were sinking and panicking and I was closer to the opening we'd crawled in through. I ripped splinters through my fingers trying to grab onto an old board and pull us in. His life belonged to me.

He kneels in front of me, "Here, give me your boots. I'll pull them off." A bottle of apricot whiskey appears like something left by a hobo. It tastes of wild leaves that curl and brown in my mouth. It tastes of 104 degrees and the flamingo and Mesopotamia crow and Tonto kneeling over the body of an Iraqi. The man's skull is split and Tonto gets his spoon out and pretends to eat his brains. Boyd snaps a pic.

I'm barefoot and my socks are in Moses' hand. "These feel like cobwebs," he says.

"I'm not in the mood."

"Just wait." He turns on the TV keeping the sound down and switches off the overhead light. The blue static is candlelight, and then he undresses down to the patch of fuzz between his breastbones, the black curls between his legs. "I want to look at you," he says, unbuttoning me. When he tries to take my shirt I hold on. No, I keep shaking my head. The stump is private. I let him unzip me and lift my legs and ease down my jeans. "Lift your right foot," he tells me. I do it.

Three men in their long dishdashas do as they're ordered. Hands tied behind their back, they wait by the roadside as their car is searched, and the gray oven world stretches in every baked direction. The soldier holds his assault weapon on the men in flowing desert clothes. He appears alien, as a grasshopper Andromeda in his neck armor, his body armor, his knee pads, and helmet and night vision goggles resting there, his Ray Bans, his desert boots. His hands, gloved with the fingers cut out and his naked chin are the only places where his weakness is revealed. That he is made of skin and tissue. "Sergeant, look what I motherfreaking found." Soldiers clamor toward the car trunk AK-47s aimed. I wait with Goliath ready to detonate or defuse. From the trunk a sheep lifts its head and baahs, a bush of fleece and weak pink eyes like cherries floating in cream. All of us high-tech soldiers crack up laughing.

Moses pulls the pillow from under the bedspread and tucks it under me. His head falls against mine. I stare at the ceiling. The room starts to go away, the TV flickers, a world without sound. Chills zigzag over the mattress when he scratches the back of my neck with his fingernails. "How about a massage?" He squeezes my neck above my shirt collar and I flinch, biting my lip. The shrapnel hit nerve thickets. We lay side by side running our fingers together. His chest rises and falls. He studies me. Like in the old days when he whittled the shape of my body into wood. His knuckles brush the inside of my thighs. My flesh thinks it's being tested, that he's just another doctor. His finger frames the red eye above my left breast. The chest tube scar.

"These are your souvenirs."

I whimper. My rib cage wants to climb out of me.

He kisses my mouth. "Close your eyes."

No. I need to see what he's looking at.

"Trust me. Close your eyes."

He arches above me, his hair falling into my face. When he pulls the shirt away from me it feels like he is peeling away my skin. His tongue flits over my shoulder and down my left upper arm, each place his tongue lights is a surprise. I roll over onto it, grab a pillow, shove it under. "You can have anything but that."

"You're a solider, right? Stop acting like a little girl." He rolls over onto his side and punches his pillow; his brows meet over his nose and his forehead furrows. "I'm trying to show you it doesn't matter. That you're still my baby."

I hear the oaks shivering in the ice outside.

"I'm pissed at the Army you left me for. Look at what they did to you," he says.

I am thinking of the three of us, running with our mutt Black Dog, through the ditches, trying to find standing water deep enough to get wet in. Frightening the bullfrogs with our kicks. Later that summer Black Dog's ears were festered with wood ticks so engorged with blood they hung like fat gray grapes. Lillian screamed that she couldn't look, they made her sick. Moses and I took lard and painstakingly eased the feelers free of Black Dog's ear and smashed the ticks on the sidewalk with a hammer until it looked like a blood asteroid had crashed.

I hear the crackle of gravel in the parking lot, a car pulling in. "Do you want this? I don't want you to be scared," he asks. "I'll stop if I'm hurting you." In the hospital they don't stop. In the Army they don't stop. I want to be kids again in the slough, spitting twigs at him. Moses moves the pillows to the foot of the bed, his hands running over the insides of my thighs. "Honey, you got it coming. No pun intended." He lowers his head, wedges my legs open. I'm creamy. That thing doesn't have its own mind; its just butter and mud. He tongues me, flicking in one spot. He licks me, nibbles like he's going to eat without using his teeth.

I push his head away. I don't want to feel.

He gets up and goes into the bathroom. I hear him rummaging. "Here," he says, handing me a miniature whiskey like a baby bottle for a lamb. "Drink the whole bottle in one shot."

I let the liquor roll down my throat. Hot like an ice cube you let melt inside you. I want to be like those wild dogs we used to see in the hay field after the baler had been through. The air yellow and sweaty, sun-splintered chaff hanging. The bitch yelping and dragging her hind legs until she was mounted. The male dog biting the loose skin at the bitch's neck while he humped her. When they were done the dogs ran in opposite directions.

Moses scoots me nearer the edge of the bed. "Don't wiggle."

His hands clamp my legs, while he licks me. I'm lying in peonies, the clench of petals so sweet it draws swarms of bees. If I roll over the bees will sting me.

"Let it go, girl. You're almost there."

"Stop," I cry, looking up at the ceiling. A sheep is dead there, its pink eyes gone to fog.

He lifts his head. "Let it out."

His tongue is making me drunk. I feel giggly but not in my mouth. The soft things are talking. "Oh, God!" It's not God of the fifteen-minute sermons. I grab Moses' hair.

"Easy on the locks." He crawls up beside me.

I feel relaxed and run over like a dirt road.

Then he lies with his head on my chest, his arm over me. "My feelings haven't changed, Bethany." Moses murmurs. "You're still my thing."

Then he enters me and we make love like slow ground soaking rain. Afterwards I push his arm away; even its lightness is too heavy. Before I can tell him more about the orchard and the apples and the snow peaches he's asleep. The song *November Rain* is playing on a car radio, the car that must be parked just outside. I picture listening to Mom's radio on the farm that picked up Little Rock. Even the disc jockey announcing the time in a far away place excited me. I listen to Moses breathe. His sleep is warm as baking bread. I close my eyes.

Specialist Boyd holds the door to the shower. I barrel against it, bang my shoulder. Sergeant Tonto tries to kiss me, "Honey, let's have a little fun. " I push him away, and then I'm on the floor by the drain. "Just lie there. Can you do that? Help out your buddies. Would you let me grind?" Although I can't see it, Tonto's tongue feels sharp like a jagged bottle. He pinches my nipples, jams a thumb into my butt. "Why do you think the Army has you over here? In Vietnam they had bargirls." This is the last heated meal of a T-Rex, frozen copulation of a mastodon. Then Boyd turns me onto my stomach.

The mounds of ancient Ur. Layer upon layer of the same city in different cen-
turies. Even without air strikes the mounds shiver from Navy Hornets and
Air Force Eagles burrowing in the sky. "She's got a skinny ass," Specialist
Boyd says, slapping my cheeks. "I like my women to have a nice thick butt."
Insurgents hide themselves in the ruins they've laced with Vietnam-style daisy
chains of explosives. "Look at it. Look at it," Tonto yelps, pulling his sex out of
me, ejaculating like a fountain. The wild ass and hyena sniff me. Later they
leave and I finish my shower. I stand in the water and shake. Back in my
quarters, I unroll my sleeping bag. My body has been inside it last still I worry
that I might brush up against someone's knobby knees. I crawl in and kick the
floor flatter, I shake.

It must be hours since Moses went to sleep. I'm speeded up inside, restless. Molecules wanting to push out of my skin. It's airless as a shed inside my hand, the one that's not there. Phantom pain. Dust more explosive than gas. I pull the bottle of Demerol from my bag and gulp. I moan. In the hospital the night medicine kept me from this. Thorazine and Seconal on top of morphine. That was the warm milk the hospital served and I needed it. Hot hot, hotter, hot elbow on the hot plate, fingers in the French fry basket. If I could only open my hand, if I could pry it open, the electricity might stop. But it's not there. It's a world away. More jolts of electricity. I huddle then stretch; I push my face against the bed board. I make a fist and stuff it against my mouth. God, make it stop.

I creep into the bathroom. There isn't a shower, only a tub, the old fashioned kind. Water rots the floor under it, chunks of damp wood and soft mold float under the bathtub. I crawl in and turn on the cold water, I dunk my stump under. I let the water flow over the invisible hand. Moses. He hadn't moved at all. I pick up one of his knives. I want to stab the hand that isn't there. I swallow Demerol. Outside the sky begins to lighten into an ugly gray. The floor may help. I crawl off the bed onto the floor. Cooler. I twist and turn; I hate Moses' sleep. Then I hear someone scream. It's me. Moses is on the floor with me, "Honey, honey." He doesn't tell me it's going to be okay. He knows better. He rocks me in his arms. "I want you to love me again."

"Don't ask that," I finally answer, taking deep breaths.
"I'm asking."

I find my way to the land of sleep and dream of rocks and a chopper just as its metal skin begins to break. The sun crawls into the sky while I envision the sun setting outside Baghdad—a pillar of highway overpass against the carmine-red sky. A fireball sun cut by bandage clouds. The day dawning is the one in which our Humvee hits an IED. Sergeant Tonto explodes; Specialist Bryan loses the hearing in his right ear and suffers traumatic brain injury. I lose my left arm, and only sweet Goliath, the robot, survives intact. The one innocent.

Afternoon and we're on the street looking for food. The burning surges through my left side, I bow my head to it.

"Are you praying, baby?" Moses asks.

"I don't know."

I have on one of Moses' flannel shirts and it feels like I'm inside his skin. I wear Moses' skinny gold pinkie ring on my index. We walk arm and arm down the street. "Hey, there's something," he points.

The Tastee Freeze. An all year-round hot dog and ice cream place. We walk through the snow and sit under the awning. I tell him that when I was four years old, I wanted to be a floating ice cream cone. There was the tiny screen that banana splits came out of. An old menu peeled from the side of the stand.

"I love these places," I say.

"You're pretty easy to please but only sometimes," Moses tells me, smiling, his eyes crinkling up at the corners. Then he knocks on the screen window. "Anyone home?"

A girl slides the screen back. She's eating a jumbo golden fried shrimp. "May I take your order?"

"I'll have a vanilla cone," I say.

"Make that two."

We sit at the picnic table outside of the Tastee Freeze. Come summer we'll fish from the bridge. He points to the paper cutouts taped to the window—vanilla ice cream cone girls floating. Like plastic explosives. A car bomb packing Semtex. Body parts. Tiny icicles hang from my eyelashes. In Mr. Millard's science class we learned dripping water and millions of years had made stalactites. I hold my ice cream for a long time. I don't want it to disappear. I could tell him how the detonator felt in my fingers.

"Like this, Bethany," Moses says. "Lick it."

And then I do. It's like kissing a cold cloud.

Jürgen Becker

Correspondent

He hardly looks into the camera; it almost seems
as if he were having a discussion with himself, a correspondence
with Something on the unseen table, perhaps
with his pen or cigarette.
A light tremble of his hands ... no one knows; in any case
very nice, nothing specific, just mumbling—
What can you say?—Coldness and glances
toward the street, which is somewhat lighted
with snow; a leftover flag
blown by the wind machine. Something gigantic that slowly
disappears ... it has already disappeared, yet before
any decree. He reiterates, he can only leave
once nothing else is happening. We'll miss him.

—translated by Okla Elliott

Jessica M. Brophy

HIS BACK

the back of my Nigerian love
is smooth like banana milk.
there are no trees on his back
or chokecherry blossoms.
only a valley and ridges that ascend
to the ocean.
what if his father had been brought to Elmira Castle?
what if his mother had lasted the passage?
his sorrow could have withered into hatred.
his body could have crumbled into bone ash.
but he lays on his side
with his geographic back
and rests
confident
delicate
jubilant.

LIFESTYLE

My ex-mother-in-law comes lumbering up the metal bleachers, squeezing between folks that give her dirty looks, trying to tote two hot dogs and two drinks.

I grin when I see her.

"Get on up here, Mopsy," I holler.

She nods, but she's watching her feet to keep from falling. Her hairline's soaking wet, because it's the kind of hot out here that'll make your heart thump heavy and slow when you're just setting still. Exert yourself and you start thinking you might just flop on over and die. Finally, breathing heavy, she gets up to where I am and hands me a tall cup of Coke.

"Whoo, good God a-mighty," she says, plopping her fat butt down and setting the paper hot dog carrier between us. She puts her feet (in pink flip-flops) up on the seat in front of us and I notice she's got her a fresh manicure on them little sausage toes. Lord, I can't help but look out toward the ball field and laugh at that woman! She tickles me with them pedicures and tan legs and that hair she bleaches. About sixty years old, two-hundred-and-something pounds and still trying to be sexy.

"Thank you, Ma," I say, reaching for a hot dog. That's what I always called her, until Tyler come along and named her "Mopsy" when he was little. "How'd you know I was hungry?"

"Just figured," she says, still trying to catch her breath. She takes a long pull on her drink and wipes her forehead with her arm, squinting out at the field. "Tyler bat yet?"

I shake my head. "He's fixing to."

I hunt through the hot dog holder for a napkin, till a *thunk* causes me to look up and see a little boy from Tyler's team jogging towards first while the pitcher and another kid try to stop the ball from rolling through the grass. They get a hold of it pretty fast and manage to throw the batter out, and the crowd goes "Aaaaw." Down on the front row the batter's big baldheaded daddy jumps up with his eyes all bulging like one of them rodeo bulls out of the starting gate, acting like he's fixing to rip a hole in the chain link fence to get onto the field. "You got to *hustle* around the bases, dammit!" he yells at his kid. The daddy's a huge guy with one of them thorn tattoos around his bicep. His little boy looks like he wishes he had a rock to crawl under.

Mopsy holds her hot dog with both hands, leaning over so nothing will drip on her shirt. "You ain't seen Ricky?" she asks me, taking a bite.

"Uh-uh. Ain't looking for him, neither."

After she swallows her food she says, all choked-up like, "I don't understand that boy. I raised him better than to do you thisaway."

My eyebrows go up. "He ain't doing nothing to *me*. Tyler's the one wants him to come."

Sure enough, when Tyler gets up to bat, he scans the bleachers. I wave, but it ain't me he's looking for. He ignores me, pouting, and turns back around to wait on his pitch. Mopsy and me cheer for him, loud, but he strikes out.

"Poor little thing," she sighs.

"He'll hit one later," I tell her, and I hope it's true because he'll be hell to live with otherwise.

The game drags on a long while, until the sun sets and the air cools off. Parents start making all the little brothers and sisters stay with them in the stands because it's dark, and the kids get bored and whine and drive us all crazy. My tailbone's about numb. There's a load of wet laundry in my washing machine and I've got to stop for milk before we go home, so I'm wishing this game would hurry up.

Over to my left, some headlights slide across the concrete block wall of the concessions stand and then cut off. Ain't nobody supposed to park over there, so I cut my eyes in that direction to find out who it is. Well, it turns out to be a car I know well and have rode in many a time. It's a Miata convertible, red, and I'll tell you it looks a lot worse for wear than when I first seen it six years ago, in 2001.

Ditto for the driver, who crunches across the gravel and steps into the lighted area. She puts her hands on her hips and stares up, checking out the crowd.

I elbow Mopsy in her side. "Look."

"What," she says, still watching the game. I poke her again.

"*What*, dammit?" Then she spots Jody standing there below us. Well, Mopsy's mouth flies open. She claps it shut again and then stares from Jody back to me a couple of times, all goggle-eyed. She sets there trying to put two and two together until finally she gets this real suspicious look and says, "You reckon that hussy's coming to watch my baby play ball?"

"Hell no," I cackle. "She's looking for Ricky!"

Mopsy dies laughing, and Jody recognizes the laugh—I can tell by the way her head snaps toward the top rows. We watch her, and the truth is that she ain't really gone downhill as bad as that Miata has—she just looks *different*.

Where she used to have slow, lazy arms that'd reach out to pull you in, what she's got now is them white-knuckle fists balled up on her hips. She used to look at me and Ricky with her eyes drooped down to half-mast like a sleepy old purring cat, but now they're about to pop out of her head trying to locate that fish that keeps wiggling off her hook. And she used to talk so fancy and breathless ... *Mmmm baby, that's so good ...*

Now, when she raises her eyes and sees me and Mopsy at the top of the bleachers trying not to laugh, her voice is flatter than a run-over snake. "Hi, Dawn," she says.

She don't wait for me to answer, just turns around and marches off across the gravel again.

Real soft, so she can't hear me, I say, "Tell him we said 'hey,' if you find him."

She slams the squeaking door of that beat-up car and revs the engine so loud that people look over their shoulders to see who's showing out. Jody throws the car in reverse and backs up, fixing to *really* impress everybody, only when she puts it in drive again it makes a backfire like a big fart and goes dead right behind the concessions stand. The crowd kind of chuckles.

"Boy," I say. "She's something, ain't she?"

Mopsy laughs until all her belly rolls get to shaking.

The night I first seen that red convertible was a Friday in 2001. I come home after work to that old single-wide trailer me and Ricky used to live in—and I hated that place, by the way. It always smelt like old cooking grease and it was so old, nothing in it looked clean no matter how I scrubbed it. I'd swore before I married that I wouldn't raise my family in a trailer, but Ricky had that old dump while he was single and he insisted we stay in it and sock our money in the bank every week. Said he wanted us to save so we could *have* something someday—land or a house or whatever.

Anyway, I drove up on this one Friday after work and heard Tyler—he was just a toddler then—screaming in the trailer. I rushed in, but it wasn't nothing the matter except his daddy was giving him a haircut in the kitchen with the electric clippers. Ricky wasn't a good hair cutter neither, but he didn't like to pay for nothing we could do ourselves. Tyler looked pitiful with his hair all chopped and big tears in his eyes.

I picked him up and rocked him, trying to calm him down. Ricky must have been through cutting anyway because he didn't say nothing, just turned around and held them clippers over the trash can, using his other hand to knock the hairs aloose from it. He looked over his shoulder and give me this little wicked grin and goes, "I hooked it up tonight."

My stomach done a little flip and started a nervous burn. I shifted the baby's weight to my hip and laid my cheek on his poor little shaved head. "Who's keeping Tyler?" I asked Ricky.

He shrugged his shoulders to say it wasn't worrying him too much. "He can spend the night with Mama and them."

"Is the girl coming *here*?"

He turned around, smirking at me like I didn't have no sense. "No, she ain't coming here," he said, pulling the plug from the outlet and winding it around his hand. "Don't nobody want you to host if you live in a trailer."

I rolled my eyes. He got a kick out of using them little buzzwords like *host*. He thought we'd joined the country club or something, instead of just started screwing new people.

Host, see, meant, "Screw at our house." *Gatekeeper* was another of them words—that one meant, "One of us will screw most anybody so the other has the say-so about who we pick." And *lifestyle* was everybody's favorite. First question any of them people asked when you met was always, "How long have you been in the lifestyle?" I guess that was supposed to make it sound classy.

Ricky and me had been *in the lifestyle* since my last birthday when he'd give me a girl for a surprise present. It was a damn surprise, all right, but let me tell how it all come about.

One time, years back, he asked me if I ever had any notion about doing something with another girl. I told him it had *crossed my mind* before, which personally I think most women would admit to if they was honest. But then we started seeing a commercial on TV for this phone line out of Atlanta where people that wanted to hook up with one another could call and record a personal ad. They had categories for everything—men wanting men, women wanting women, couples for couples and what-have-you. Ricky got excited about it.

"Call them up and find you a chick to try it out with," he kept saying. But he wasn't fooling me none, acting like he wanted me to try it out of the kindness of his heart. What man did you ever hear of that didn't want to screw two girls at once?

I said, "I'll pass."

But I admit them commercials put ideas in my head. I never done nothing kinky like that and I was pretty curious about how it might be, but on the other hand it worried me to think about opening the door of our marriage and letting strangers walk in. At times I'd think *why not*, and then I'd think *no*.

Still Ricky kept bringing it up every time we seen the commercial. Finally one night I guess I got the look on my face he'd been waiting for, and he broke out in a big old satisfied grin and said, "I can *see* you wanna do it. I'm gonna fix you up."

I said, "Bullshit." That ad said the phone line was free for women but $19.95 a month for men, and anybody that bought generic beer, I figured, wasn't fixing to pop for no subscription to a phone sex line.

But what can I say—I guess I underestimated the places a man's pecker can lead him. My birthday come along—my twenty-sixth—and my husband said he was taking me on a hot date. We left Tyler with Mopsy and went over to Applebee's for supper. Big deal, right? But when we was through eating, Ricky got that little dirty grin on his face again and drove us over to the Traveler's Inn, where he parked the car and pulled out a room key that was hid in his pocket. He already had a boner in his pants.

"Oh *hell* no," I said.

He said, "Baby, I ain't gonna do nothing but watch."

I was pissed off. "Ricky, if I'm gonna do something with a girl I'd like to at least *pick* the girl," I told him.

But he started whining and acting all pathetic. "You'll like this one. It's for your birthday, baby. She's already in there waiting on you."

I fumed, wishing I had drunk a couple more margaritas at Applebee's. We had a short fight about how Ricky had found the girl and whether he'd already tried her out himself, but he swore he hadn't. So eventually, he got me to go on in the room and there was this old nervous-looking chubby girl on the bed in some jeans and a tank top. "Happy birthday," she said.

I said, "Thanks," though none too friendly-like. I felt kind of ill. But we all set around and talked awhile and she acted all right, so I made up my mind I'd try to go through with this thing and see if I could find out what women was like. First, I sent Ricky down the street for a bottle of vodka and some orange juice we could drink to loosen up. He come back with the liquor plus a deck of playing cards, so we broke the ice playing strip poker. When we'd lost a few items of clothes and drank four or five stiff drinks apiece the old girl made a move on me.

She kissed me and started feeling around on my chest at the same time, and let me tell you, it was different than them daydreams I'd been having—and not in a good way, neither. It felt so freakish it was all I could do not to slap her hand off me, but she'd no sooner got started than Ricky was saying "Oh, *yeah*," and pulling him up a chair so he could have a ringside seat. I was afraid he would have had a stroke if I'd backed out right then. There was this kind of electric, red-alert feeling in the room. Other than the air conditioner humming the only sound you could hear was that girl's mouth, on my face and my neck and then on downward, and the sound of Ricky shifting around in his chair trying to get the view from every possible angle. I felt real detached, like all this was happening to somebody else, and while she was doing various things to me I wasn't thinking nothing more than, *this is interesting, but gross*. It come to me (a little bit late, I know) that her being a woman didn't cancel out the fact that she was a *stranger*, and what we was doing just ain't nothing you ought to do with strangers.

So. I was glad when it come time to leave that motel room and that strange girl, and you would think I'd chalk the whole experience up to a lesson learned, right? But here's what's crazy: no sooner was we out of there and back home in our own bed, than what we'd did started seeming like the hottest thing in the *world*. My brain played a trick on me where once I was back at home I forgot about the mosquito bites all over the girl's legs and about how worried I was that Ricky liked her titties better than mine and all that stuff. All I remembered was that I done something wild and kinky and my husband watched me and now we was going at it like rabbits.

This kept up between me and him for weeks, so pretty soon I'd caught a little case of amnesia about how relieved I'd been to get out of that motel room and only remembered how sexy me and Ricky felt afterwards. And because I *kept* fooling myself like that, we wound up doing the same thing again and again, with different people. Ricky wasn't satisfied to be just a spectator for long, of course. He got me to feeling *guilty*, saying it didn't seem right for him not to get to do *nothing* … couldn't he just touch the girl? And then couldn't she just touch him? And then, if we're gonna do one thing then why not another, until before long we was piled up in strange beds of other couples with Ricky humping and moaning over the wife while I was splayed under the husband. That's what they call a *full, same-room swap*, if you want to know. Supposedly, them type of couples get a thrill out of watching one another with somebody else. Personally, I wasn't getting a *sexual* thrill out of none of it while it was actually happening—it was only kind of hot to look back on and think about when I was home with Ricky.

This was a confusing time in our marriage. Half the time we was electrified with this wild secret that we didn't dare talk about to nobody. It was like a roller coaster ride where the queasy feeling of watching my husband with somebody else got mixed up with the feeling that to be able to *stand* watching must mean we was a special couple with a marriage so strong that nobody could ever come between us no matter what they was offering. Another part of it that kept me off-balance was that the little spark of having new men appreciate what I had to offer—you know, all the stuff Ricky didn't notice about me no more—maybe *would* have been fun, had it not been for me feeling like my husband was mighty willing to trade me off. So like I said, half the time we was electrified, but the other half the time we was getting into situations that made me feel like the scum of the earth.

One time I'll never forget. We was spending the night with this couple at their house, and we'd grilled steaks and ate baked potatoes and all, and just set around talking and drinking like normal folks. They had this little girl that was about four or five and they kept asking her all night wasn't she tired? Wasn't she ready to go to bed? Finally she conked out in front of the TV, and her mama said us grown people could get the party started. Me and her went in the bedroom to put on our lingerie but of course we wound up staying in there and then of course the husbands followed and all the usual groping and grunting took place.

I never could fall asleep after it was over. The rest of them did, but I laid until the sun come up and then put my clothes on and went to their kitchen to find me something to drink. My head was aching. I opened their refrigerator hunting a Coke and when I shut the door, there stood their little girl with her thumb in her mouth. I must have jumped a foot off the floor.

"You scared me," I said. My heart was pounding from adrenaline, plus from hoping she hadn't checked her parents' room first and seen Ricky in there. I made myself smile at her, though. "Your mama's still asleep."

She looked like she wasn't surprised. "Will you fix me some breakfast?" she asked me.

I give her what she wanted, a bowl of cereal and some apple juice, but I felt like crying. Little kids ought not to have to wake up and ask strangers to fix their breakfast. While she was eating, I went down the hall and made Ricky get up.

I woke the mama up, too, to tell her we was leaving and her child was awake. She rolled over and said, "Okay, baby. I'll call you later." I wouldn't be surprised if that little girl set there by herself all day while they slept, and that wasn't right.

"Ricky, this is trashy," I said, when I was driving away from their house. He had wadded up his jacket for a pillow and was trying to go back to sleep. I told him, "I ain't doing this no more."

He just laughed. "You ain't fixing to quit. That'd be like going to Baskin-Robbins and ordering vanilla every time."

"That's why you get married—because you like vanilla!" I hollered. "You ain't supposed to want nothing else!" But that wasn't really the point I was meaning to make, so I tried to quiet down. "I promised myself I wouldn't grow up to be trash," I told him. "That's one of the main goals of my life."

He raised one butt cheek and farted, so I just let my window down and quit trying to talk to him. He was snoring in a couple of minutes.

On the drive home I done a lot of thinking about how I'd swore not to be like my parents was. They wasn't fit to have kids—couldn't never hold a job or provide nothing for me and my sisters. And then a memory come to me that I hadn't thought of in years, about this one time when my family was staying in somebody's *garage*. I was in there by myself one hot evening—well, my little sister was with me but she was asleep—and the man that lived in the house called me to come in and look at the news on TV, because John Wayne had died. He acted all tore up like it was somebody he knew personally. I didn't hardly know or care who John Wayne was, myself, but after the news went on to other stories the old man give me some cookies so I was just setting there enjoying the air conditioning. I was about six or seven, just setting there on the sofa eating Oreos and wondering if I could take some for my sister, when that man says, "Dawn, look here at this." Well I looked over at him and he had undid his pants and had his old pecker sticking straight up out of them.

I didn't think twice about nothing. "That's nasty," I said. I stood up and threw them two cookies I still had right on his living room floor. "You old nasty buzzard."

I run right back into that hot garage and slammed the kitchen door behind me, and I looked for someplace to hide but he never actually made no move to come after me, so far as I could tell. When my mama and daddy come in later, I told what happened.

My daddy clenched up his jaw and made fists out of his hands. "Well," he said, not looking me in the face, "you ain't hurt." He seemed like he didn't want to hear no more about what I was saying.

And my mama looked kind of sad but she just said, "Baby, we ain't got no place else to move."

Trashy. That's what that was. I swore I wouldn't never grow up to be like them, not having a pot to piss in and having to leave my kids in the hands of God knows what kind of freaks. *Well, I ain't as bad as they was*, I was thinking as I turned the car into our trailer park. *We've got a place to live and some money in the bank, and Tyler ain't being exposed to nothing bad.* Then it hit me that *I* was the sex freak somebody else's child had been left in the hands of, and I knew this getting naked with strangers business was not how I wanted to live.

After that night, I didn't intend to ever swing no more, but I'm ashamed to say that after some time, we drifted back into it. We done it for the same reasons everybody else probably does—cheap thrills. We didn't have no boat to ride around the lake, we didn't have no plane to hop on or no vacation house, but when we couldn't take the same-old, same-old of life no more, we could always swing. *What the hell*, we figured at them times. It give our batteries a charge for a while, and at least we wasn't doing drugs.

We decided to quit the couples and stick to single girls, when we could get them, but it pissed Ricky off that the ones I picked always latched onto me more than him. That was only because girls can get a man anytime, but he complained until I threw up my hands and said, "Fine. You find one." And this brings us back to that night in 2001 when I come home and he said he'd fixed us up with a girl that turned out to be Jody.

Here's how it went. Me and him had a strategy about first meetings where we'd always asked the girls to meet us at this catfish restaurant that had a front door and a side door. Then we always tried to set at the first high-top table in the bar and watch the parking lot for somebody that fit the description of whoever we was meeting. If they was too nasty, we could slip out that side door before we ever got tangled up with them. It don't sound nice, I know, but we figured it was kinder to let people think they got stood up than to tell them to their face you wouldn't have them. So there we set at the first table, watching for Jody.

"Can't miss a red convertible," Ricky was saying.

Personally, I was betting we was getting scammed, because when I heard an ad that sounded as good as hers did, I figured why would this person need to use a chat line to meet people? She claimed she was tall and sexy and built like a brick shithouse, besides driving a red convertible. I was thinking *yeah, right,* but Ricky was lit up like a kid on Christmas.

I was drumming my fingers on the table, waiting until we could go home, when Ricky said, "Here she comes."

That Red Miata, brand new back then, had whipped into the parking lot and the girl in it was parking and climbing out. Ricky give me a smug look like *See there?* and for the first time since we started this stuff I felt a cold kind of fear in my stomach, because she looked the way her ad claimed and then some—tall, killer body, dressed perfect. Tan, with long glossy dark hair. I was gonna feel like shit beside her, but then I realized—she was probably gonna turn *us* down. We wasn't nowhere in her league.

"I will tear her *up*," Ricky whispered to me.

Jody come in the door, looked over at us and smiled. She knowed us from our ad and the description Ricky'd give her, so she come on over and climbed up on the swivel chair beside me and said, "Hey."

My husband fell all over himself, going to the bar to get her a drink—couldn't even wait for the waitress to come. He *paid* for it, too, and that was one for the history books, but Jody just laughed at him and paid all her attention to me. Within a little while, she had me feeling fairly comfortable, but then, swingers have kind of a behavior code about how you handle a couple. It sounds crazy, but the thing is that you don't never want to make nobody jealous. You might be fixing to *screw* their partner, but you ain't supposed to act like you *like* them or nothing. I wasn't sure if maybe she was being extra-friendly to me just because that's the way it's done.

We chit-chatted a while and asked her what she done for a living and all. She grinned and said she was a teacher. "Now guess where."

We couldn't guess, so she giggled and said, "Mount Olive Christian," and then hid her face with her hands like she was ashamed of herself, but died laughing at the same time.

"*Christian* school?" Ricky said, looking shocked. I just set back in my chair and studied her like you would an interesting bug.

"Oh, God, I can't help it," she said, laughing and stretching. "I was sincerely a Christian when I got the job, and in six months I might be sincere again. But right now—"she put her hand on my leg—"here I am."

"Damn, let's get the check," Ricky said.

I took it for a joke, but Jody goes, "Okay," and smiled and me and then at him.

She lived in the Tree Hills Apartments, and when I seen her place that first night, it was so pretty it made me want to choke Ricky for the dump he had us living in. Jody unlocked her door and waved us inside, where she had clean white walls with modern-looking pictures on them and tan carpet and central heat and air. She had a matching tan leather sofa and loveseat and a glass-topped coffee table with *fresh flowers* on it—now who would think of buying fresh flowers for their living room? The air smelt like her perfume.

"Real nice place," Ricky said, and then excused himself to the bathroom.

I set down on the sofa, trying to hide my purse, which I noticed had become tacky all of a sudden. Jody kicked her high heels off into a corner. "Nine West," the label in them said, and looking at them made me realize my *shoes* was tacky, too. One had a nick on the heel that I colored in with a black marker and never thought twice about until then.

"Let's see what we can drink," she said, smiling at me and going into her kitchen. Her lips was made up berry red. I set there not saying nothing while she looked in the fridge, and in a minute she took out a bottle of something light green and got three glasses out of a cabinet.

She come back and set down by me, putting the stuff on the coffee table. "Do you like appletinis?"

I said we hadn't tried them. Ricky was still in the bathroom, now running water. I was betting he was maybe trying to brush his teeth with his finger or something to make an extra-good impression.

Jody poured me a drink and I reached out for it, kind of stiff.

"Smile!" she said all of a sudden. "I know you can't be *this* nervous." Then she got a worried look and set the bottle down. "Don't you like me?"

Considering what we was there for, it sounded so sad and childish I got tickled at her and laughed. "I like you," I said. Then I decided to just come on out with it. "We never done this with somebody so gorgeous before."

"Oh," she said. "Thank you," and tossed her hair over her shoulder like it wasn't nothing to be so pretty you intimidated people. She went back to pouring drinks for her and Ricky, and when hers was ready she clinked it against mine. "To new friends."

We both drunk a swallow, with her looking at me the whole time. "I think you're beautiful, too," she said, real quiet. She cut her eyes toward the bathroom and goes, "No offense, but I wouldn't have gone ahead with this if it was just your husband. You're the one I want to play with."

See, that's how she was. Hadn't known her an hour and she was already messing with my mind. Ricky come out of the bathroom grinning all goofy, and for the first time, he embarrassed me just like my purse and shoes done. Before that night it had always felt like me and him on one team and then the new person on another, but Jody divided us.

For months after that night, we was all disrupted. I never did know why, whether it was something particular that attracted her to us or whether she was just a real needy person, but she wasn't like the normal swinger that just wanted to meet up and party once in a while. No, she wanted to be our best friend. I couldn't hardly get home from work good every day before she was knocking at the door of our trailer. I'd be folding clothes or cooking supper or something, and she'd follow me around, chattering until my head ached. She wanted us to get facials or manicures; she wanted me to go shopping with her and compliment her about everything she tried on. She called me at my job most every day when she got a chance, and on Fridays she'd say, "So what are we doing this weekend?" like she took it for granted that whatever we was doing, she was going with us. And she always wanted to be entertained. I mean, there's nights when all you want to do is take a bath and get to bed early, but there we'd set on the sofa—tired out from a day's work, Ricky with the remote in his hand and Tyler already asleep on my chest—and Jody'd give a big sigh of boredom and say, "Let's *do* something."

Unfortunately what she wanted to do was never the activity that Ricky was hoping for, which wore his patience real thin. Here he had found her himself and things still didn't work out to suit him. He was about insane with wanting to have more sex with her but she wasn't coming across with any—what she wanted to do was have lunch or go to the mall with me, but when we did she embarrassed me by trying to buy me things.

"I'll get it for you," she'd say if I stopped to look at anything.

Of course, I'd tell her no but then she'd look at me like I was pitiful. "You should have more," she used to say. "I'll tell Ricky to get it for you."

Then I'd die laughing and explain to her a few facts about Ricky and his spending habits.

Finally, after another one of them torturous days at the mall (where she walked ahead of me and looked at herself in every single store window) I cut ties with her. I had come to realize it wasn't no accident that she picked out people like us who was, you might say, "beneath" her. I think it made her feel like a star. All I felt was like I was being imposed on and I knew it was time to get rid of her. Ricky didn't want me to—he about cried every time I hinted like I was wanting to give her the boot, but it didn't make no sense to me that I should be stuck hanging out with her all the time and stroking her ego, just in case he might wind up getting laid. I wasn't his damn pimp. So I told Jody, nice as I could, why things wasn't working out no more. She went all to pieces about what a friend she'd tried to be to us and then blew up, blubbering, "You only wanted me for sex!"

"We wasn't advertising for friends," I told her, and that was the plain truth.

Well, sometimes you look back on things and wish you'd done different, and sometimes you look back and wish you hadn't done them at all. Here's how things turned out with Jody.

A couple of weeks after I cut her off, me and Tyler come home from a family reunion one Saturday afternoon, went down the hall to the bedroom and found Jody in my bed with Ricky. I covered Tyler's eyes and run out of the trailer, feeling so amazed it's a wonder I didn't trip over my bottom lip.

When you swing with your husband, see, it's like you have a pot of gold and you're saying to other women, "Now there's plenty of gold here and I'll be glad to share it if you just ask." When that's the situation, you know that only a lowdown dog would go behind your back and steal it. I can't even get into what kind of a retarded husband would cheat on a wife that lets him screw other women anyway. Damn if *that* ain't biting the hand that feeds you.

I knew Jody was trying to hurt me for rejecting her, and Ricky was just thinking with his wiener like men always do. But things have a way of happening, and I thought I seen an opportunity to get out of that trailer. I stayed with my cousin for a couple of days after what happened, but then I went and took half the money out of me and Ricky's savings account. It wasn't enough for no house or land or nothing, but I got me an apartment with clean white walls and my own tan carpet. I got me some furniture, and a flowery comforter for my bed and one of them fancy shower-curtains with the tiebacks on the side. I got one of them racecar beds for Tyler, and it made me so happy every afternoon when I turned the key and walked into that cool, fresh-painted place. I was just like the Jeffersons, moving on up.

I thought Ricky would see how nice our family could live and join us shortly, and I still think he would have if Jody hadn't wound up dependant on him. But right at first, just after I moved out, he followed his pecker to Jody's place and started spending every night with her—finally doing, I reckon, what he'd been so keyed up to do all those months when she aggravating the stew out of *me*. Now that he was her chosen one, he thought he was living large, and believe you me he wasn't refusing anything she wanted to buy him. I seen him uptown with different stuff—NASCAR jackets, gold chains. After a while, he started looking kind of dazed.

Mopsy was tore up. She'd always said if Ricky and me ever split up she was keeping me and disowning him, and she wasn't hardly kidding. Tyler and me still see a lot more of her than Ricky does, but she hears from him enough to pass me the news, which is how I heard about Jody getting fired from her job. A single teacher at Mt. Olive Christian was on the Internet looking for a boyfriend I guess, and found an old ad Jody posted, hunting men, women, or couples. It had a skimpy-dressed picture of her with it, and the school principal called her into his office and fired her right in the middle of a school day. *Moral turpitude*, he said. No other Christian school would touch her and even if a public school might have, she didn't have the credentials to teach in one, so she lost her pretty apartment had to move with Ricky to the trailer. She got her a job at a bookstore eventually, but they're still to this day living there in the old grease-trap. Mopsy says Ricky's got them both socking their money in the bank, so they can have something someday.

When Tyler and me get home from the ball field it's nearly ten o'clock but I tell him to take a shower anyway because being clean is one of the items on my list. When I realized I'd be raising him by myself, I set down and made up an actual list of ways to not be trashy. It's got like fifty things on it.

He's been in a so-so mood since we left the game, because he did get some good hits and score some runs, but his team lost anyway and his daddy never showed up. He sets at the dinette table, swiveling his chair back and forth instead of going on into the bathroom to do what I told him.

"I know one good thing, Mama," he says. "At least I ain't got a daddy like Josh's, that hollers at me when I do bad."

My washer and dryer are in a closet right beside my dining area and I'm putting the wet laundry in to dry. "That's the truth." I say. I think about it for a minute and have to laugh. "Sometimes I guess we can just be glad of what we ain't got."

I make him go on and start his shower, and while he's in there I get me a bottle of water from the refrigerator and set down on the sofa to see what's on TV. A Lifetime movie looks pretty good—real dramatic—so I stop there and put my feet up on the coffee table.

There ain't no more drama in my life. I work at my job and take care of my son, and spend my nights and weekends at the ball field. My parents wouldn't have never paid for my sisters and me to play a sport but I do it for Tyler even if I have to go without something for myself. Ricky don't come around much, but I don't care. What kind of nasty influence would he be on a little boy? There ain't no man in my life and I sure don't want no woman. I might not never be able get me a house or any land. But times like this, little minutes of peace and quiet, I look around at my little apartment and take a minute, like Tyler done, to be glad for all the things I ain't got.

Jan Pettit

I need to break laws

But I'm not stupid. I don't walk
the black ice of the creek
or press my tongue to every metal pipe—
though danger loves my defects.
It used to be food—hell, it still is.
I tried to eat myself, starting with my toes
then hands and hair. Some days,
I'm the worst kind of ungrateful.

What was missing was so small, like a thin coin
lifted from a box of treasure. No one should
have noticed. But here we are, damaged
in such spectacular ways—an extra eye,
a breast chewed off, the cleaver
in the head. My mother says,
if you're going to write tributes to me
please don't wait until I'm dead.

But the middle child's role is to disappoint
over and over, and under
the ice, something beautiful wants finding—
the fish mythmakers have died
trying to describe, the way it swallows moonlight…
all you have to do is capture it, slit the belly.
Find out what was done, what was not.

Jan Pettit

Everything must go

Nothing can be content with idleness,
not squirrels or robins or clouds—
which we expect to pass in front of the moon,
build fluffy animals and pose for science photos
when they have spare time.
Everything must go.
We cannot keep last year's children
or Sunday's leftovers any longer—
old newspapers, half-empty medicine bottles,
everything must go.
No junkers in the front yard, please,
don't drive in if you can't also drive out—
flat tires are useless to us. Everything
must go—surely your mother told you this?
Before they were called slackers, they were thinkers.
Artist is a word for fail. Unbusy hands
find matches, learn to masturbate.
Stillness is like practicing for death.
Frankly, that's why we have a problem with trees:
they refuse to go,
and when they do it's always trouble.

SLEEP APNEA

That's me behind the wheel, head thrust forward,
over the limit in my 280Z, in a rush to Lake City

where he's drunk down at the Oak Room,
Budweiser lifted in his hand, then dropped like an ax.

Together we are a window shade unsprung,
mattress ticking pressed into the sides of a face.

Next thing, we're two martinis sleepwalking,
taking Polk and Geary at a tilt, groping at fog.

That must be some other woman in copper taffeta
polka dots, pursed lips, missing the punch line.

Then came the year of loss: the cat, the ovaries, the him.
He stood me up for *Marshmallows! How did you know?*

the Jungian symbol for fuck you. There's just not
that much good sex left in the world. When it's dark at four,

who can say how much is normal? Please wake me.
Every now and then, I forget to breathe.

Claire Ibarra

A Glimpse of Color

The mother had been gone for a long time. She was a painter and had decided that she needed to know intimately the colors of the Mediterranean Sea; a painter could not paint without a deep, personal bond with that body of water. Now, as she explored the daughter's cottage facing the North Atlantic Ocean, she knew she had been right. She already missed the view from that little house in Llanqa, a village tucked along the coast of southern Spain.

The daughter spent her days working in a bookstore in town, and while she was away the mother would snoop, peeping into boxes and drawers and cabinets throughout the cottage. She didn't think it was spying—she just wanted to understand the woman the daughter had become. After noticing the stacks of books about Buddhism on the daughter's nightstand, the mother asked her, "So, are you a Buddhist?"

"I like it; it makes sense to me, but I don't meditate. I guess I'm not."

In the mother's family they were mostly artists. The mother recognized the oil painting done by her great-grandmother when she was eighty-six years old, the watercolor of a single oak tree painted by her uncle, several photographs of erotic flowers taken by her brother. The mother's father had been a woodworker, and there were several pieces of antique furniture he had restored: the daughter's dresser, a framed mirror, and a round mahogany table hidden under piles of bills and coffee mugs and books. The mother was surprised she had left behind all those family relics. The items made the daughter feel connected to a family.

The mother especially liked that the daughter hung a picture she had painted in the center of the living room. It was an impressionistic oil painting of the daughter when she was young. The mother had dressed her in a sunhat with feathers and flowers and a lacy dress and she was barefoot sitting on decaying wooden steps in a garden. "I'm glad you have the painting," the mother said.

The daughter had always known that the painting was not meant for her; it was meant to make the mother a successful artist. The art dealer told the mother it was a nice painting, but the market was flooded with impressionistic posters—there was nothing to be done. It never became a poster hung in the living rooms of many people; it was only one painting that hung in a little seaside cottage.

Another day, the mother examined the large map with little pins stuck everywhere, which leaned against the wall. She was surprised that the daughter had traveled so much.

That evening, they had dinner on the deck—facing the gray, foamy water—and the mother said, "You have traveled all over the world."

"Some people call it wanderlust. It was hard for me to settle down, but I've lived here a long time now and don't feel like going anywhere. A walk along the beach seems to be enough."

"I traveled throughout Europe, and my favorite place was Greece. The colors in that country are marvelous. Photographers, painters, poets, they all flock there for inspiration." The mother was trying to impress the daughter.

The daughter had been to Greece. She had enjoyed the friendliness and charm of the people, the fresh flavors of tomatoes and feta cheese, and the impact of violent volcanic forces on nature, but she didn't feel like mentioning it to the mother.

There were a lot of things she didn't feel like mentioning, such as that she enjoyed writing. She didn't consider herself to be a writer, she just liked to make up stories about people and their lives. She had been engaged once, but it ended before marriage—and she yearned to have children but now believed it was too late.

Instead, she asked, "What are your plans?"

The mother stared out at the turbulent ocean—the white caps flipping like large seagulls—her eyes became dark and narrow. The mother realized it was strange for her to have just shown up there without warning or an explanation. She had been gone for so long. "I have no plans; I just wanted to see you."

The daughter felt a little sorry. "Well, you can stay for as long as you like. I'm not going anywhere." The daughter rose and collected their plates dappled with bits of leftover salad and baguette crumbs and took the dishes into the kitchen. The mother didn't offer to help.

The daughter began to wash the dishes in the old ceramic sink, stained with yellow rust and chipped at the edges. Over the sink was a window with a view of the dunes with long pale beach grass, beige sand and the gray waters. It was soothing, the calm faded palette of colors that faced the daughter every day. Even the sky was always a dull shade of blue, hardly blue at all. If I were a painter, I would use these palettes of color—only hints of color, barely discernable, she thought.

The daughter went back outside wearing a wool sweater and sat in an old wooden chair made comfortable by damp, moldy cushions. She could tell the mother was impatient, yearning for something more exciting and alive and colorful like other seas in far away places. The mother wanted to hear music and see dancing. "Remember when your father used to play flamenco on his classical guitar? When you were a child you used to dance and keep rhythm with castanets."

"Yes, I remember. That was before you left." And the daughter remembered that the father never played the guitar after that.

On Sunday the daughter decided to take a walk on the beach. It was a cloudy day, and she wore rubber boots and carried a spading shovel and bucket. "I'm going clam digging in the tidal mud flats. You can come."

"Do you clam dig often? Is it a hobby?" The mother asked, curious to know more about the daughter.

"I like it; it's relaxing."

"How do you do it? What does one need to know to dig for clams?"

They were on the deck, facing the water, and the daughter thought for a moment.

"There's not much you need to know. You look for holes in the muddy sand; it's where they draw in and expel water—for eating and breathing. Dig gently to avoid breaking their soft shell. Replace the small ones under a thin layer of sand so that they are protected, but too much sand will smother them."

"How did you learn so much about clams?"

"From a book."

"You know, I think you are a Buddhist," the mother said thoughtfully.

The mother decided to stay at home. She preferred to watch the beach from a short distance away than actually make physical contact with it—all the sand that sticks on everything was a nuisance, and the wind made the mother feel too flighty. The mother didn't know it, but she was that way with a lot of things: admiring from a short distance.

She watched the daughter walk down the beach, until she became just a blurred speckle. The mother could barely see the daughter walk into the tidal flats and kneel. She could see the bright yellow of the boots she wore and the green of the bucket. The mother always saw colors.

A few hours later, the daughter was walking up the rotting, loose steps, which led from the sand dunes to her deck. She was wet and her long hair was a tangled mess and she smelled like the ocean. The mother thought she looked like a real seaman. The daughter set down the bucket and it was half full with clams.

"Would you like a cup of tea?" the mother asked.

The daughter didn't answer because she was watching an old man walking along the beach. It began to rain lightly.

"Who is that?" the mother asked.

"I don't know his name, but he walks by every day. It's strange that I don't know his name. He's always barefoot and in the same clothes."

The mother noticed his yellowish-white hair and dark-tanned skin. He wore a black t-shirt and black shorts and carried a twisted, knotty walking stick. He didn't look up at them as he passed by, just kept his head facing the ocean.

"Just like the old man and the sea. He looks homeless."

"Perhaps he is." The daughter didn't want to ask the mother if she was homeless too. The daughter didn't feel like worrying about cooking another nice meal. She wanted to eat cheese and crackers, while curled up in her bed, and watch a movie—a movie with Cary Grant. "So, what shall we do now?"

The mother knew she was a bother, just showing up after all these years. She didn't even know why she came, but now she seemed to be stuck. She couldn't figure out what she was supposed to do. I am alone, she thought.

The daughter was alone, too. Somehow, they both had ended up alone.

The next morning, the daughter knew that the mother had left. There was a space within the cottage that had been occupied, but now the daughter could feel it empty. There was a note on the kitchen table which thanked her for everything, and which also told her: it isn't good to spend too much time alone. You should invite the old man for a clambake—isn't that what you're supposed to do with clams? What does the book say?

The daughter was surprised that the impressionistic painting was still there. She thought it would be a temptation for the mother, all those rich colors, and the blues of the sky and of the flowers looked just like a sea from a far away place. But there it hung in the very same place, just as it had for many years.

Claire Zoghb

THE RELATIVITY OF DISTANCE

My car noses upward on the bridge in Bourne
into mottled pearly-grey clouds. Below, the
canal lies flat and wrinkled, a satin sheet the color
of gunmetal slipped off a bed to the floor.
Fond of edges, I head to where the Cape
raises its scrawny arm between ocean and bay,
where scrub pines grow low enough to whisper
syllables. He flies in the opposite direction, into
furnace heat and floods of a Texas August. How
odd distance is—sometimes I lose his face across
the nautical miles of his tea cup. But tonight I will
turn westward in my sleep, spoon him until
sun-up, make of the grand Mississippi a single
rivulet of sweat coursing down his back.

JUST IN CASE

Marn 11

Mch 11

Spring is historically in the black. Ten more days; I can't wait. Paul Dexter at *Forbes.com* wrings his hands about the lack of volume. I know it will come with the flowers and the volume can only lift the mid caps, the small caps, the penny stocks. The large caps are toast, I think, one way or another. Until then the market can't sustain much over a two or three percent rally before it pulls back. But money can even be made in the mud. Especially in the mud.

I do all of this for my family. That's what they forget sometimes. Chloe and Edwin and Candice—my life. They simply have to let me do my thing.

It's after four and I have CNBC on, of course, and I'm scanning my usual post-trading suspects: *The Motley Fool, Fortune.com, Smart Money, The Street.com, Yahoo Finance*, various blogs. Then at 5:00 I click back through my holdings to see if any news came through the AP wires. For now I'm checking the message boards. The shorts are bloodsuckers. Thieves, those idiots. I circle the purple band.

I glance out the window at the rectangles of siding. My view: completed units clustered together on what used to be my family farm—on the cow pasture, to be precise. The capital the developers threw our way was just far too sweet to pass up. So we caved. One condition, I told them: we stay put right here in the farmhouse. Build around us. They hemmed and hawed, but in the end we shook hands, signed papers. Just like that; it was done. They managed to spin it: "The rustic farmhouse preserved at the hub of Meadow Haven offers a nostalgic glimpse into the roots of Loudoun County." I don't memorize much, but that one is scorched into my cerebral cortex. I like how they included "preserved," as if this phrase was their idea. I say "they." Can't bring myself to even mention the developers' names.

I look away.

By five luckily it will be too dark to see anything but lights. I imagine those as planets, moons, stars. It's much tougher in the day.

I immerse myself in several articles on power picks.

At six, the mutual funds report their gains/losses. I go back and click, scan my Yahoo page. I have traded most of my mutual funds for ETFs. It's easier, quicker to buy and sell on the minute. No load, no fees. I'm in full. I do some long-term trading, some mid-term, and a healthy dose of day-trading. I've got a million in Diyani, an ethanol stock. Ethanol stocks are the new dot-coms. There are others besides Diyani, but Diyani is the one worth watching. Unlike the dot-coms, though, there is a real need for fuel. The market is there, the P/E will follow.

For tomorrow I decide to stay put—for *now*. I can hear Chloe call me from downstairs. It's dinner. I circle the purple rubber band around my wrist, as usual, and lock up my office. Personally, I can't stand the thought of even a family member in there in my absence.

Edwin sits on an old Loudoun phone book, and Candice kicks him under the table. Six and thirteen. These are good numbers.

I say grace and my wife holds my hand. We eat the chicken parmesan she prepared, the mashed potatoes, string beans, salad. It's a fair approximation of an all-American meal. I'm a lucky man.

I ask them about school.

"Mom," Candice says. "Can I be a fire-eater?"

"What did Mr. Lucas teach you today?"

"Nothing. I'm talking to Aimee about the circus and she says she saw a fire-eater—or breather. I forget which. What's the difference?"

"It might be both," I say.

"The answer is no," Chloe says. "Look, the circus is fun to watch, but it doesn't pay, and the conditions are horrible. It's not a good place for a girl to be." Chloe glares at Edwin, who makes to grab Candice's chicken. This is normal behavior.

"The circus isn't a *place*," Candice says. She leans forward for emphasis. I wonder if her friends call her "Candy." I hope not, for evident reasons. I could accept "Can," but even that rings of a bordello.

I know Candice loves me, but I have to wonder why she approaches her mother rather than me with important life decisions. Am I overly detached, or is it a gender thing? I write it off as the latter.

After dinner, I try to help Candice with her homework, but she locks her bedroom door on me. She says if she's not joining the circus, she's not doing a stick of homework. She says it's a free country. We all do.

March 21

Chloe says the house looks "run down." I could hire a crew of college students to do some routine maintenance, but I'm stubborn. I know it. Chloe tends to obsess about paint chips and water damage. It's fine. Plus, even if it isn't, the mere fact of its unsightliness pleases me: anything to give the developers some acid indigestion. By seven I've read *The Times* Business section, *The Wall Street Journal*, more online pieces. I've also entered a few stocks into my Excel spreadsheet: I don't leave a speck of this to guesswork.

This is the first day of spring, but the Dow is down over seven percent in the last week. My gut is battling my head. I know my weakness: fear is difficult to combat. And it's no walk in the park to feel optimistic when I'm bleeding eighty, ninety grand a day. My head tells me to crunch the numbers, focus on the technical analysis, P/E ratios, EPS, debt, revenue growth, total cash. There is such a thing as rational analysis. Though I disagree with his buy and hold strategy, Warren Buffet's level-headed approach helps. So does stoicism: fear and greed both wash over the market. The key is knowing when you have a sound buy regardless. Hold your ground, even head upstream.

I post comments on the message boards all day, sniping with the shorts, validating the longs and seeking validation. One of the guys who goes by "Frank Finance" posts a message on an ETF site about selling the market short—how he wished he had, to be more specific.

"No way," I write. "I don't care if we're in a 1929-like crash. I'm never turning bloodsucker. It's un-American."

This provokes some vitriolic responses from the shorts, to put it mildly.

By noon the Dow is down another two and a half-percent. I decide to bail—profit or no profit. My number crunching is telling me we might not hit this level again in years. I hop onto E*TRADE, sell half my individual positions and a third of my ETFs. Since I don't have a hedge (no bonds either), everything is way down. I wince. My gut churns, but I know it's the right thing to do. I'll buy everything back when the market regains a foothold. Then I'll stake out my profit. By my analysis, however, that might not be for a while. I hold onto the rest for safe-keeping, or because I lost too much I can only hope to regain.

I discard the now-unlucky rubber band and pick another. There's a difference between a paper loss and a real loss, which the less savvy investor loses sight of. This one's in six figure territory.

At 12:30 Chloe brings me my usual: tuna on rye, small baggie of pretzels, a bosc pear. It's a sweet gesture. The floor creaks as she shifts her weight.

"Can I eat with you today?" I ask. "Do you mind?" I feel squinty and want a break from the rivulet of numbers.

"Oh, okay. Of course," she says. This was likely the last thing she expected me to say. She knows me. "That's fine."

We sit at the kitchen table together. Chloe doesn't eat, but she drinks tea and watches me. I lean over my food and shovel it in without dignity. I've built up an appetite fighting for my dime.

"How's the tuna?"

"Tasty," I say. And it is. (She's chopped up bits of chive and cucumber and olives into it. I love that.) The subtext is everything. She knows better than to ask how the market is going today. I'm sure she can tell by watching my face. It's not difficult. I can feel her reading me.

"What have you been doing?"

"Working on the closets," she says. Her life is so straightforward compared to mine; I envy her. "Reorganizing a bit. Going to the store later. Need anything special?"

"More rubber bands," I say. "Same kind. Maybe that will help."

I down my water, thump the glass back on the table.

I'm back at my computer in ten minutes. The S&P is down sixty-five points.

I used to love to play cards in high school, in college. We'd bet pennies on rounds of five-card draw. That was good. I could play all night.

Watching the market get socked once again, I decide my strategy might need adjusting. To recoup my losses I might need to focus more intently on penny stocks. No risk, no reward, I think. Steady hand. Both feet on the ground.

I close up shop at two. By this point Chloe is out buying eggs and milk. I open the front door and sit on the porch. The air is cold and dry and a slight breeze whistles through the scraggly saplings the developers planted here and there. Red maple. Dogwood. Luckily the farmhouse still backs to real woods. It's not old growth exactly, but it's older than anything else around here. There's a creek back there and a culvert—it's of no use to the developers. Wetlands. This is surely one of the reasons the house and the immediate yard was of less concern to them than the pastures around it. They'd only get one unit out of the land at any rate. I watch the Garnet's white plastic grill cover catch the wind. It reminds me of Marilyn Monroe's skirt. I'm not immune to simple beauty, I just have no interest in the people who now live in my cow pasture, in what was.

As the youngest among my siblings, I always suspected I'd missed the boat, that I was born too late. My sister Henrietta and my brother Joe seemed built of a better substance somehow. Growing up, I felt I constantly had to prove myself to them, that I needed to become famous or strike it rich or marry a Hollywood princess. I don't know why. Henrietta and Joe were perfectly decent siblings, not abnormally competitive. Maybe I felt as if I needed to prove myself to my parents, because they had such sound temperaments. My father was a farmer all his life. My mother was what they call a "homemaker" these days, and in many ways she was a simple, content woman. It's difficult to look back at my life without growing nostalgic. I had a wonderful childhood. Everybody should grow up on a farm.

March 22

It's nine and I'm watching the numbers on the pre-market. I've been at the computer for six hours already. When trading is hot and heavy I can't sleep. Actually I usually can't sleep without a brandy and fifteen milligrams of Ambien.

I'm out of lucky rubber bands. Each one I try has nothing. No mojo. Nothing. The bands Chloe bought for me aren't right—wrong color, wrong thickness. I can't get comfortable. Pre-market the NASDAQ is getting pummeled. The Dow and S&P are no great shakes either. This is where my breathing exercises come in. I inhale, count to ten, exhale, count to ten. I gnaw on my bar of dry Ramen noodles, drink coffee, click refresh every ten seconds or so, cross my fingers. The pre-market is down with each click.

I try to tell myself that the pre-market can be deceiving. The volume is low. It's not an absolute indicator, but it's something. It's *an* indicator.

By the opening bell everything I own is getting hammered. I'm forced to resort to my stop-loss strategy and sell off. Too much capital at stake. It's a fire sale. Just about everything I own is back into the cash reserves in my E*TRADE account. The only individual stocks I hold onto are my ethanol plays; they are fairly steady. My mantra: Ethanol=the new dot-coms. Repeat. Repeat. This time no bubble. I'm not going to stop riding the wave.

Chloe brings in my lunch and doesn't say a word. Good. I nod and keep plugging through, trying to figure this thing out. I'm set on making this work. If the developers can buy up my cow pasture, I can buy low and sell high. I'm determined.

Rather than fiddle with my lunch for two hours, I gulp it down in five minutes, swallow a glass of water. Back to the computer.

On the message boards the shorts are having a field day. Dire predictions are all over the blogs and financial sites.

My breathing quickens and I restrain it. One through ten.

I decide on a bold move, but one that will likely recoup my losses: I'll put all three mil on Diyani at two dollars and sixteen cents. It's a can't miss, really. The stock was up to seventeen last fall and only fell in the fourth quarter on specious rumors and mediocre-but-not-poor earnings. But what didn't fall in the fourth quarter? What didn't show poor fourth-quarter earnings? Insider buying is sky-high, and the company has the makings of impressive fundamentals. Even the pickers say Diyani is a solid play. It's up from ninety-six cents in January. I've bought and sold it several times now, and managed some sizable gains.

Don't buy on emotion, I tell myself. Don't get carried away.

I enter the symbol, the shares, the price type. I look at the numbers, hesitate. What if the support for this stock erodes? What if another nebulous rumor plagues the stock? Then I'll sell. If it dips, I'll sell. I'm not an idiot. Day traders don't buy and hold. It's in and out, in and out. Only if I see a huge coup will I hold. Otherwise I'm not sticking around. But it has to be a pretty endless wave, a big kahuna.

I click the button for "place order." I feel confident.

After I make the purchase I click refresh every five seconds until four. The stock goes down two hundredths of a percent, then up two hundredths of a percent. I close up shop.

Before dinner I go on a rubber band hunt. After searching four stores I finally find the thick purple bands at a craft shop. I buy two bags.

That night Chloe gives me the once over about the windows, the gutters, the yard. I made promises, she says, and I keep saying "I will," but I don't. I'm shamed; she's right. She shouldn't have to do it all. Then she's into me for disappointing Candice. I want to tell her. It's just...

"Her soccer game. It was right there on the calendar," she says. Chloe went from running errands to the game, and I was supposed to meet them there. I was wrapped up in my after-hours technical analysis, seeing if I could find another Diyani out there, just in case. It's always just in case. I lie in bed on my back, unable to sleep. Guilt burrows into me. Chloe drifts off in a snap; I'm left there jittery and anxious. I hate taking sleep medicine. I always wake up with that hangover feeling. Less energy for trading.

I take it anyway.

March 23

I can see the crocuses, the green daffodil spears ready to bloom. It's spring. The market is still getting walloped. At *Fortune* they're underplaying it, calling it a "correction." Everywhere else they're calling it a downright crash.

I quickly check the pre-market on Diyani but nothing shows. I'm better off; I'm terrified to look. I figure I can sacrifice a morning, do chores. It will sharpen my thinking to take a break. I clean the winter debris from the gutters, wash the outside windows, pick up fallen limbs, rake the winter leftovers. When I was a kid I loved to be out here. I could spend all day down by the creek, skipping stones, watching minnows. Despite my protests to my mother, I particularly loved clearing away the limbs from the yard. I could whack a stick against a trunk all day—fighting invisible dragons.

I find myself lost in reverie back there, away from the computer, away from modern-day Loudoun with its McMansions and quarter-acre lots of straw and grass seed, filler chinaberries and hackberries that replaced the century-old oaks they turned into wood chips.

By the opening bell I'm back at my computer, firing up CNBC. I'm thinking how nice it feels to be focused on just one stock. I never knew how much time I spent wrestling with my basket of holdings. Now I don't have to.

When the numbers come up, my gut drops. "Holy shit!" The Dow is down four hundred points, the NASDAQ two hundred. I log onto my computer, check Diyani. Chloe is out grocery shopping again.

Down seventy-five cents.

Down eighty-five cents.

Down a dollar. Fifty percent.

What do I do?

It's a bloodbath. I discard my rubber band, try another.

With a downward move of this magnitude I can't sell. It would be stupid to sell. If I had money on the side I'd be buying like crazy. But even I might hesitate with this kind of move. I'm sure there are hundreds of bargains out there though. But losing a million and a half on paper—you can't sell into that movement.

I just can't watch. I shut the computer down. Unplug the cord. Turn off the monitor. Turn off the television. Unplug that cord. It's fifty-five outside—clear and almost balmy. But now I don't feel like working. I want distraction. I descend into the basement and unearth an old edition of *Webster's Dictionary*. To relax I read definitions. I pull out a lawn chair and make myself a cup of tea, and I read definitions all morning and into the afternoon. By then Chloe is back, though with only a single bag of groceries.

"I had some other things I needed to do," she says. "It's a long story." She walks off upstairs.

I tell her I need to use the bathroom.

Checking Diyani again is a bad idea: the stock is down another ten percent, under a buck. The shorts are all over the board. The morale of the longs seems crushed. I log back off and throw away the rubber band I have. Then I empty both bags onto my desk. I cut each rubber band in half with scissors and dispose of the pile. Ignore the street, I tell myself. Block the hype from your mind. The stock will find buyers.

At the grocery store I find a suitable single band around a bundle of green onions. I decide on this alternative route. I buy two more bundles, just in case.

I have the urge to bond with my daughter, play cards with my son. After dinner this time Candice lets me help her with her homework. My son and I play Go Fish. The last thing I want to do now is read anything containing the word "finance."

I do my best to make our bedroom romantic: candles, wine, lulling Beethoven nocturnes. Chloe shrinks from my touch.

"I just want some alone time," she says. "It's been hectic."

I try to not appear wounded. So I don't say a thing.

"Is everything okay? You seem...I don't know." She crosses her arms, says she feels a chill.

I don't want to talk about Diyani. I don't want to even think about Diyani.

"Sure," I say. "Everything will be fine." Chloe's face squinches at this, but she grabs a stack of magazines, sways off to the den. The kids are in bed. I eat a bowl of applesauce to settle my stomach. I take my Ambien. I know sooner or later I have to face my fears.

March 30

When I wake up I'm astounded to see Diyani still at twenty-seven cents. I'm so used to seeing it dwindle by now, if it even holds steady at the next day's opening bell it'll be some kind of relief.

I've lost all hope of Diyani recovering to anywhere near two dollars. By now I'd settle for a dollar—even eighty five cents. If I can recoup somewhere near a million, we can still live comfortably for the rest of our lives. Pulling out at less than seventy cents would be a catastrophe. I know this.

I'm so used to sleep deprivation now I can barely remember what it actually felt like to sleep through the night—at least without twenty milligrams of Ambien. I'm used to diarrhea, depression. I haven't made love to Chloe since spring began. Honestly, I can't remember the last time. Even on the occasions when she's ready and willing, I don't have any luck down there. Everything rides with Diyani.

Rubber bands are out. It's paperclips now. I've tried gold-plated, silver, pink, purple, yellow. I'm on red today. It's in my pocket. As I'm reading *The Wall Street Journal*, I have my paperclip in the other hand.

I've begun praying. I'm not a religious man.

I have to excuse myself from breakfast to vomit in the bathroom sink. When I'm done I splash myself with water.

At ten I log on. The Dow is up two percent. I see that right away. But Diyani is down another eight cents. The message board is all but silent. The insider selling is through the roof. More rumors of liquidation are bleeding in through the wires.

I log back off, shut down the computer. Chloe knows something is wrong by now. She also knows she shouldn't ask me questions. She should have done that a long time back.

I go for a drive, out Meadow Haven, west on 7. It takes almost an hour to reach the pasture land—what's not pocked with development. The county is quickly becoming urban, just another strip mall on the way to somewhere else. At Hillsboro, I take Mountain Road up to

Britain, head to the river. In the pastures, cows loll by stands of oak and walnut, and out in the open. The grass is greener each day. The cherry trees are almost in bloom. I ignore the new, hulking buildings.

I wish I had more friends. Advice would help: I am not sure what it is a man is supposed to do in this situation. As it stands, my options are slim.

I park on the shoulder of Britain Road. I lean against the fence, watch the cows. All I'm thinking is I hope these people never sell. When it grows dark, I limp back to the car, turn the ignition, listen to the engine. I drive home.

After the kids are asleep I tell her about Diyani. She doesn't scream. She doesn't cry. This is not her style.

"You were going through this the entire time?"

"Yes, I was." I can't bring myself to look at her. She continues as if I didn't respond.

"And you didn't talk to me about this." She blinks, stunned by her own observation. I know this bit strikes her to the core. For her, keeping secrets is antithetical to our marriage. Still, I suspect she has kept things from me for years. I just don't know what. I feel her eyes glaze over me, watching my every move.

She whispers, "What will we do?" I tell her we'll have to wait— that Diyani will come back, that the market has really stumbled.

"I've messed up," I say. "I know. But it's all on paper. It's temporary."

"When does the paper become not just paper?"

I lack an adequate answer for this.

July 3

It has taken three months plus, but we've finally sold the house. Despite the fact that the mortgage was paid off in 1973, we could no longer afford to live there with zero income. When Diyani declared bankruptcy on May 1st, there was little I could do. On my taxes I will declare the loss of three million, one hundred thousand, three dollars, and sixty-two cents. I'm not sure what this will recoup, but it will surely give someone at the IRS a story to tell over dinner.

I don't pity myself. I've been through that. I'm fortunate to be married to the most loving woman in Loudoun County. She calls my loss a "family matter"—meaning my family. It took a while for me to actually believe she was able to forgive me. In some ways I am still skeptical, but she says she's not angry.

"I'm disappointed," she says. "Saddened you wouldn't think to come to me about this."

And she's confused. Chloe thinks we need a break. Next week I'm moving to a one bedroom apartment in Harper's Ferry. This is a temporary measure, she says, until I "regain my balance." After that we'll see. My sister thinks I should hire a lawyer "just in case." I will begin to write down what Chloe says; I know that. I have thought about tape-recording her when she is at her most generous.

I applied for an assistant manager's position at a fast-food burger joint, and the regional manager says I have a "decent shot." I've always enjoyed the smell of beef sizzling on a grill. I guess I've come full circle. Since the house sold I have enough money to live on for a while. The buyers are, of course, going to tear down the family house and build a McMansion, in keeping with the rest of Meadow Haven. I just need to keep my mind occupied. I'm only forty. I have a long way to go.

As for the computer, it's going to my nephew. That's a certainty. I can't even enter my office for the physical pain it causes me to see it. Out of sight, out of mind.

My sister wanted to get away from Northern Virginia for exactly this reason: she felt that the Washington area was going in the wrong direction, that it emphasized the most superficial aspects of life—money, power, status. Henrietta argued that DC's suit-and-tie mentality was at odds with the rural past of its surrounding areas. From the time she left in 1992, she thought the area was only going downhill—more people, more developments, more congestion, worse traffic. Joe disagreed. He left because he simply didn't want anything to do with the farm, the land—except the cut he received when our father died. My mother was forty when I was born, and she died at seventy one. My father made it a few years more, but he was miserable shuffling about the house, doing his own laundry, cooking his meals for the first time in his life. After she died, they should have put him down like an old dog.

Before we finally moved I walked through the development, my wife and children next to me. I wanted to see the homes for what they were. I looked at the thin brick facades, the small lots, the immensity of the homes themselves. The homes seemed so cheaply built though: if I blew hard enough I imagined half would tumble to the ground. This is what it has come to, I thought. We are being pushed out by people who don't even have the sense to purchase a decent structure. This is the ultimate triumph of money over brains, I thought.

I said hello to the few people watering their lawns and walking their dogs. One blond couple watched their daughter bounce up and down on a trampoline. I watched her ponytail flog her shoulders with each bounce. A man taught his son to shoot a free-throw. His son hunched down in an exaggerated crouch, bending his knees. An old woman planted orange marigolds in a flower bed along her front walk. You are the lucky few, I thought. I tried to smile, count blessings, all that. I only hope my children can remember this land the way it was...before. I will. I know it.

Teri Ellen Cross

WRATH
—for Yvette Cade and other women who have felt it

First I feel the wetness, sudden,
spreading like shame saturating
my blouse, my skirt, my slip.
The smell of gasoline washes
over me like an overpowering cologne.
I realize the origin, the Sprite bottle
in my estranged husband's hand.
I think, *Roger I will get to you*
in just a moment, I have a customer waiting.
Then I hear the whir and click
of the lighter and heat leans into
me for a kiss. Flame eats the air
from his hand to my skirt, my blouse,
my bra, flame eating its way to my
face like a hungry lover's mouth.
A new smell, at once familiar,
unnerving: burning hair.
Heat's breath is in my face.
My face is melting, dripping
into my hands. Now, as flames
lick my ears, Roger opens his mouth:
Bitch, how pretty are you now?

Ryan Stone

CATCHING EARL

Once a week, on Wednesday, Ted goes to his group. It's a group about control, controlling anger and aggression and rage, all balled up in the basement of the First Methodist Church. It's run by a little, scrawny guy named Ernie who distributes weak orange soda. Orange soda. In the basement of the Methodist church. How can this be salvation, Ted often thinks, and he looks at the soda can and at the other men listening to Ernie and feels a little silly sitting there. Then he thinks of Marie at home with her burn scars from sometime when he lost control and turns his soda can over and over in his hand and tries to stay focused.

Earl and Susan live in Ted's neighborhood, across the street. Ted can see their one-story ranch through the crab apple tree in his front yard. There's a small, tipped-over tricycle in the driveway. Ted believes Earl beats Susan. He believes this because of the way he's seen Susan act. Susan is guarded, always hunkered down and tired looking as if she gets no sleep. And Earl? Earl is quiet enough, but there's something about him—perhaps it's his eyes, or all the flannel he wears that makes Ted think he's up to something.

It's more about Susan though. When he looks at Susan he sees Marie's younger self. It was when he realized Marie had lost her will that he fought the urge to fly off the handle, joined the group, and told her things would get better. She'd lost her will to fight when their son, Danny, left for the Marines. He is fighting in a war now. Ted and Marie, their battles long fought, often sit in the living room, look at the pictures of him in his uniform, and cry at the thought of his possible death. Earl has a young daughter named Melissa, and they see her out on the front lawn every now and then, playing beneath the walnut trees and riding her tricycle alone down the middle of the street. Ted's perception of the situation across the street annoys him so much he figures if he says something it will, at the most, make him feel a little better, which is the only thing anyway.

Wednesday night, Ernie challenges them with the old fall-into-your-partners'-arms game. They've played this one before, but Ernie says it's important to constantly reintroduce trust. Ted wonders how he will catch the monster he's paired with. The man weighs about two-seventy or so and none of it muscle. Ted thinks about Earl and how he would fit in here. He looks much like the rest of them—small men, with small eyes and balding heads, except for the younger ones who have slick hair or thin beards. Ted throws himself backwards into massive arms. His eyes are closed. He's so close to losing his trust in everything that he's nauseated. He feels the room spin, the black behind his eyes pulses, and Steak catches him. They call the heavy man Steak because that's what he likes to eat and talk about. He's always talking about the steak his wife used to fix him.

Ted wonders if Earl could accomplish any of this, or if he's so far gone it's not worth it, but Ted can't get any of it out of his head—how Earl's wife and daughter cry when he comes home and how that sound can come right across the street, like a neighbor's leaves, and through his windows, into his and Marie's life while they are trying to contemplate the existence, dead or alive, of their son. Steak lets him go.

"Now me," he says and turns. Ted can not see around him, and Steak is crossing his arms. Ted has a vision of letting him fall and the ruckus that would cause, the commotion, but he's not sure he wants to piss Steak off. So he reaches out. The big guy falls back and Ted catches him, but as he does, he falls backwards, slipping, and his wrists slam back as they hit the concrete floor and arch toward his forearms, jamming them. Pain ricochets through his arms, his wrists throb, but he pushes up. As Steak comes to a stand, Ted rolls on the floor, rubbing his wrists. Ted fumbles around, trying to get up. Steak offers him a hand, trying to preserve trust, but to no avail because when something bigger than you asks you to trust it, it's just a little too damn heavy.

On Saturday, Ted meets Earl on the sidewalk. They are both walking their dogs. Earl has his little schnauzer on a short leash. Ted walks his bull terrier. They exchange pleasantries and talk about the oncoming fall, how the leaves will cover their yards, and how those Chinese chestnuts from Dan Davies' yard will spill out all over the neighborhood, carried by wind and squirrels, and the sharp thorns will stick their feet. They laugh at this.

Earl wears a red flannel shirt tucked in at the waist and jeans. He looks ready for hunting or a Lands End catalog shoot. Ted is in his bathrobe because he feels comfortable in his neighborhood now, feels as if he can walk around in his bathrobe. He's lived here twenty-two years—he's earned the right. And besides, people don't look at him anymore anyway. They know about him, about how he used to be with the binge drinking and the job loss and the beatings, but now he's different. Now he's a sad old man in his bathrobe, and he likes the idea of that. It makes him feel as if he is one with the neighborhood. Earl is still young and can't walk around in a bathrobe. He has to be trimmed and proper. Earl tells Ted he's having a party this weekend to watch the football game.

He mentions something about moving forward, putting his life back together, and then says, "I'm only inviting a few people, but why don't you stop by. Just the guys. I'm buying the beer."

Ted thinks for a moment. Next Sunday. What is he doing next Sunday? Since he's been sober he has trouble remembering what his plans are, but he knows it's only because he *has* plans. He can't think of anything and wonders what it will be like to see the inside of Earl's house. He's afraid it might be too familiar, but he decides he can take it when Earl presses. It's only a football game, after all, and even though he cares little for football, it's the local pro team, and that might be enough to catch his interest.

That Wednesday, Ernie asks about his son.
"Do you know where he is?" Ernie asks.
"No," Ted says.
"And how do you feel about that?"

This is one of Ernie's favorite things to do, make people sweat with questions that have no real answers. Questions that are so complicated they give Ted a dull ache on the bridge of his nose. He answers this one the same way he answers all of them.

"I don't know," he says. Ted feels rage about it. It makes him hot underneath his clothes. It makes him feel as if he's never been able to really understand anything that goes on inside his own house, even after he quit drinking, and that makes him hot. How can his son walk off and never return? He doesn't know, of course, that he won't return, but he knows he'll never see him again, just as sure as he knows that Ernie's questions will make his nose hurt.

"Work on that," Ernie tells him. Then to the rest of the group, "We've got to understand ourselves before we can begin to understand what limits us."

Ted is not stupid. He knows Ernie believes that he sobered up because Danny left but that it also dug a vacant hole in his life. Ernie believes each of them has lost something, like a son or a mother, and they need to reconnect with that loss on some level. These are the things he tells them when he meets with them one-on-one in the church office. He places his degrees from the University of Phoenix on the desk in frames leaned against stacks of books with titles like *Finding Your Inner Child* and *The Lost and Hopeful*. When he meets with Ted, Ted doesn't say much but does tell skinny Ernie how things are with Marie. Things are better, he tells him each time. Today we went on a picnic, or a walk, or something to do with nature because Ernie likes to hear this. Whether or not he's actually done something like that really doesn't matter to Ted, but he knows things are better in some ways. He wonders what Earl would say in a meeting like that, if Earl would respond the same way.

Ted turns his warming can of soda over. Droplets gather around his fingers making his hands clammy. Ernie is pairing them off. It's time to discuss the feelings they've had this week. Steak is paired with someone else, and Ted gets an angry, bald, little runt of a guy named Peter who is twenty-seven, but looks much older.

"I got so mad this week at Phil," he's saying. Peter is gay and Phil fills him up. "I was so mad I broke our Tiffany lamp. Can you imagine? I just broke it. Right there on the floor in front of him. He was so sad, and I love when he's sad. It makes him look like one of those pound puppies and makes me feel so good. Do you think that's why I broke the lamp? Because I like him like a pound puppy?"

"Yes," Ted says.

Peter leans back in his chair, crosses his ankles, and looks content. "What about you? Did you commit any crimes this week?"

But Ted says nothing.

Ted shows up at Earl's place. He's the last one to arrive. Dan Davies is there, sitting in the overstuffed easy chair, and one of the guys who works at the little gas station at the block's end. There are only four people there, including Earl, and when he comes in he's wearing a sweatshirt that says "Rams" on the front. He offers Ted a beer. It's an import called Damm.

"Drink all the Damm beer you want," Earl says with a laugh. Ted takes the beer, settles in on the couch between Davies and the filling station guy and they turn the game on.

"We're playing San Francisco," Earl announces to no one. He drinks and his moustache spreads over the top of the can, curling over.

"Are they good?" Ted asks. He feels a little misplaced here amongst these younger men—men with vigor, men who don't need a hot shower each morning just to work their joints out. They all look at him at the same time, as if he's the kid in class with the stupid question. He sinks back into the couch again and wonders why in the hell he accepted the invite in the first place.

"They're all right," Davies says. Davies is closest to his age. He was at least alive in the sixties, and Ted thinks this gives them a bit of a connection.

The game goes forward. And when St. Louis scores they all jump up and high five each other. Ted tries, but he's late standing up, and by the time he's risen, the rest have sat back down. He doesn't understand the game. The strategy they keep talking about is beyond him. And though he knows how football is scored, it's difficult to keep track of each team's points. Instead he looks out the window and sees, across the street, his own house, tiny and situated right on the corner, hidden by the sprawling crab apple tree. The tree blooms once a year in spring, and when it flowers it smells wonderful, like sweet apple spice, and the blooms are light pink, the color of a baby's cheeks. It's the prettiest tree on the block, but it only lasts for two weeks and then, as if it's lost interest or attention, it goes blank.

Behind it, he can see the house and thinks of Marie. She's baking a pie today, peach, and will have it done when he gets home. Baking takes up a lot of her time. He can see his windows. They are dark, even in the daylight, and he can't see in them. He wishes he could so he could have some kind of contact with something familiar. St. Louis scores again and he's on top of it this time, up and high fiving them all around. When he sits back down his back aches.

The game ends, and Davies says, "That's a winner," and leaves without saying goodbye. No one seems to notice or care.

The filling station guy leaves, and it's down to two. Ted sits with Earl in the living room, watching the television. The couch is plaid and covered in a bright orange afghan and this afghan itches. Ted reaches to scratch his back, as he does Earl stands up and moves toward the door.

"Damn Chinese chestnuts," he says. The door's open. They can see the yard.

"Yeah," Ted says. "Say," he says, "how are things with you and Susan?"

The question feels ridiculous. What business is it of his? Susan hasn't been there the whole time. She took off for the grocery before the game started. She'd left before Ted made his way over, but he'd watched her from his window, hidden behind the shade, and she'd had a couple of plastic bags with her, and her purse, and a book, so wherever she was she was probably comfortable for now.

"Things are okay," Earl says. He comes back, sits next to Ted. "I guess."

"You know," Ted says, "I've heard you guys sometimes."

"Yeah?"

"Sure. It's pretty loud. I'm wondering what the other neighbors might think. If they might call the cops? What do you think?"

Ted isn't sure if Earl knows about his past. He wasn't around for it, but it may have made its way to him. Ted's past tends to follow him that way, through the tongues of others who had the experience.

Earl straightens up. "It's okay. We fight. A little. It's pretty stressful around here right now." He turns off the television and stares into the screen. "I mean, everything that's gone on." He straightens up, squares his shoulders. "I'm supposed to put things back together. That's what this weekend was about. Sort of."

Ted remembers a time when he saw Earl and Susan out on their front lawn screaming at one another, making a large scene, and Melissa was there, crying. It was awful. "You should talk to someone," he says.

"We fight. I mean what do you expect?"

Ted isn't sure if this is directed at him.

"I mean with what's happened and all," Earl says.

"I meet with these folks, once a week, down at the church. We sit around and talk. That's all. We have a beer, or two," Ted lies. "And we talk. That's all."

"What do you talk about?"

"You know. How to be in a relationship. How to be yourself. That kind of stuff. You have to understand yourself before you can understand your limits."

Earl gives him a funny half-smile.

"Why don't you come with me next week? It's not that bad you know."

The age gap between them hovers over Ted's head. How could this young kid, this young man who has a job in construction, who knows how to build things so they come out right, listen to an old, shaky man who wanders around the neighborhood in his bathrobe, who doesn't like to be noticed, who would rather sit in a soft chair and stare at the wall thinking about his son? How could those two people ever meet somewhere in the middle, or at First Methodist for that matter, and come up with the answers? But, Ted thinks, here I am, sitting here on the young man's couch and really trying to reach out, trying to make things better for someone else. Maybe, Ted thinks, I'm getting better.

Earl says, "Can Susan and I both go?"

"It's for men only," Ted says. "I'll come by on Wednesday and see if you're ready. If not, you can wait. You have to go on your own terms." Ted finds himself echoing Ernie more and more, as if the man is taking up residence in the side pocket of his brain.

"That's fine," Earl says. "Thanks for coming. Good game, huh?"

Ted looks down at the television. "Yeah, good game. Around seven o'clock, then?" Ted says. Then he says, "I don't care much for football." As he's walking home, Susan's car turns onto the street heading for home, and as they pass him, Melissa, in the backseat, waves at him. Susan has the window down and has the radio up very loud. Brown paper sacks are piled in the back seat around Melissa. He can see this as they drive slowly by, and he can hear the music, some rock from the seventies, "Jim Dandy," and he's glad he's not wearing his bathrobe.

He can't wait to get home and tell Marie about the thing he's done today, about the steps he's taken. There's a jump in his walk, something he hasn't felt for a long time, and it makes him a little uneasy at first, but then he falls in line as the song comes back to him. *Jim Dandy to the rescue. Jim Dandy to the rescue. Go Jim Dandy. Go Jim Dandy.* Marie will be proud of him.

He shows up a little early that Wednesday, wearing his khaki slacks and navy blue sports coat and loafers. There are white specks on his shoulder and he brushes them off. Earl is on his couch, and Susan is next to him. They are both looking into a blank television set, staring at the reflection staring back at them. Because they don't see him, Ted pauses before he knocks on the glass door. They look lonely there, with the cushions and a mound of silence between them. He notices Melissa is in front of them, cross-legged on the floor, and she is staring at the blank television as well. There are pictures on top, family photos, Earl's family all together, close knit. There are some of them with a young boy in the photo, some without. Ted knocks and disrupts the scene. Earl lets him in.

"You're early," Earl says.

"I'm sorry. It's just that I'm excited about this for some reason."

"It's all right," Earl says. "We're just finishing up here."

Ted smiles and nods at Susan and Melissa, who nod back. They are both lovely looking, each with dark, silk brown hair and big eyes, so dark there's no apparent pupil, and this is a little haunting but at the same time enticing. It drags him right into their stare.

Earl speaks over his shoulder. "When I get back we'll watch Jake's video, okay, the one with him walking across the living room?"

"All right," Susan says. "We haven't watched video in a while."

Earl goes out, and after a wave to the women, Ted goes, too. He wonders if Earl has told them where he's going and asks him this as they climb into Ted's Volvo.

"No," he says. "I'm going to see how it all pans out. Then I might tell them. If it helps."

They drive to the church. The leaves are on the ground now, spread out under the trees, all brown. Mixed amidst them are Chinese chestnuts, littered around the street with spindly, dry hulls. The church is not far. They say little on the way outside of boring remarks about the weather.

At the church, Ernie sits them all in a circle, as he always does, and passes out the soda. One for each, he says, just like each week, and Earl gives Ted a look of disappointment—the kind you give the bad waitress. Ernie begins by telling them about his week. He's had a few problems at home this week. The gutters are falling off his house, and he has this squirrel problem. The little shits keep eating his pecans. Some laugh as he tells it, but Ted can see it bothers Ernie because he keeps looking down as he says these things. He's not really talking about the squirrels. They all know that because, in his weaker moments, when he's not feeling up to leading the group, Ernie breaks down about his wife, Linda, who died in the car crash. Ernie did time and now that he's out, leading the group is part of his recovery. He shows them his tattoos sometimes.

"Now," he says, "who would like to go first?" He goes around the circle with his eyes. Each man looks at the ground, until he gets to a man named Raphael, who looks right at him. "How about you Raph?"

Raphael stands up. "So, I'm going to get the paper this morning, and this kid rides by on his bike, right? And this kid, he says 'Hey mister, get the fuck outta my way.' And I'm thinking, 'What the hell?' and this kid, right, he says, 'Get the fuck outta my way.' I took him off that bike and popped him in the nose, is what I did, see. Or what I woulda like to done, see. I didn't do it cause it isn't right, but I woulda liked to." Raphael sits down. Ernie gives him an approving smile. It's tough to get a hold on what Ernie thinks. He has a way of smiling that takes over and doesn't let out what he really believes. Ted hates this. Earl is next.

"You're new to the group, yes?" Ernie says.

"Yeah."

"Why don't you introduce yourself to everyone."

He hesitates. "I'm Earl. Earl Dobson. I came with Ted."

The group, in unison, says, "Hi Earl."

"And why have you decided to join us?" Ernie asks.

"I guess to work on my marriage."

"Whose marriage?"

And the group says, in unison, "*Our* marriage."

Ernie says to Earl, "You need to recognize the cooperation between two people. That two people exist in your world and your actions hurt or help both of them."

Earl gives Ernie the same look Ted got when the soda was handed out.

"Four," Earl says.

Ernie looks at him, his face blank.

Earl says, "There are four people in my life."

"Good," Ernie says, "who's next?"

Steak is next. Steak stands up and gives a long winded description of an argument he had with his girlfriend, Wanda, which escalated, but was then brought down to a discussion level. Ernie applauds when he finishes. They go around the circle. Ted had a few stories he cooked up when he started the group, and he rotates them weekly. It's not that he

SUBSCRIBE TO *NATURAL BRIDGE*:

One-Year subscription $15* ___
Two-Year subscription $25* ___
Back Issues $5 _ Issue ___ Copies: ___
*institutional, $18 1yr/ $30/2yrs
*add $5 for foreign

Support *Natural Bridge* with your donation:

Donor ($25-$99) ___
Patron ($100-$250) ___
Benefactor ($250 up) ___

Name: _____
Address: _____
City: _____State: ___ ZIP:_____

Please indicate if this is a Gift Subscription. [ ]

Please make checks payable to *Natural Bridge*.

We are online at www.umsl.edu/~natural
email: natural@umsl.edu   phone: 314.516.7327

Natural Bridge ~ English Dept. ~ One University Blvd
St. Louis, MO 63121-4499

doesn't want something to tell, it's only that he has nothing. When he told Marie about helping Earl, Marie had taken his hand, led him to the couch, and sat him down. She pointed to the picture of Danny and said, "Look with me. Look at him." And they had sat on the couch for the next hour looking at the picture. Danny's uniform looked tight in the picture, wrapped on him like a glove.

The time comes for the trust fall exercise. They partner up, and Ted is expecting Steak again, but he gets Earl. They stand on the far side of the room, away from everyone else.

"Look," Earl says, "this is a little embarrassing. What's this all about?"

"Control," Ted says.

"Control? Over what?"

"Over yourself." Ted wants to ask him about him and his wife and daughter staring at the blank television set, but doesn't.

"I have control," Earl says.

"I know," Ted says. "I know you do."

"Why do people think I'm out of control? My boss thinks I'm out of control, tells me to take a few days off. My sister thinks I'm out of control, tells me not to call her anymore. My father *is* out of control, and he thinks *I'm* out of control. What the hell?"

"We should do the exercise," Ted says.

"What is it?"

"You stand here," he says, pointing in front of him, "and fall back into my arms and I'm supposed to catch you." Earl gives him the look again, only this time he cocks his eyebrow.

"That's it?"

"Yes."

"This is what you do?"

"Yes."

Earl shakes his head and takes his position in front of Ted. "I should go home," he says, "and be with my son. We're going to watch his video tonight. The one where he's walking across the living room. It was the first time." Earl moves in front of Ted. "I got the video on the first time. I wonder how many people can say that?"

"Cross your arms," Ted says. "It makes it easier to catch you."

Earl does. He stands in front of Ted, crosses his arms, and his shoulder blades sprout out of his shirt, little triangles. Ted can see around him, unlike Steak, and he can see the rest of the men falling into one another's arms, over and over, and enjoying it, laughing and giggling like high school kids. It's a big game, he thinks, just one big game. He reaches down and rubs his jammed wrist. It still hurts a bit. Earl looks back at him.

"Now close your eyes," Ted says. Earl turns his head back. "Okay, whenever you're ready."

Earl falls, arching back and into Ted's arms where he lands against Ted's stomach. Ted reaches out and wraps his arms around Earl, feeling the man's weight sink against him, feeling the push against his spine as he digs in his heels, but Earl begins to slip, falling, sliding out from under his fingers. Losing his balance, Ted stumbles back, slipping on the shiny linoleum floor. They tumble, both of them, to the ground.

Boris Vian

THE PRIEST IN SWIM TRUNKS

The Priest in Swim Trunks, originally published in *La rue* July 1946, is the title story of 15 Stories by Boris Vian 10/18 Christian Bourgois Editions. Paris, France, 1988.

I blamed it on Pawels. Without his money I'd never have gone to the Deligny swimming pool and nothing would have happened. I wanted to look at the girls, and to tell the truth I was fortunate to pass unnoticed. I'm not a card, but being an ordinary joker I do have all my equipment as well as a tan (due to a bad liver).

It was pleasant in the shade trees. I didn't dare go swimming. Pawels scared me with his sun-bleached skin. Besides, I had women to ogle. But as luck would have it they were bad-looking.

I laid on my back. My eyes were closed and I waited to turn totally dark. Just the moment I was forced to turn onto my stomach so I wouldn't look like a striped beach awning, some guy reading a breviary tripped over me. Hell-o, it was a priest. So priests swim too, I thought. And then I remembered the Seminary Code only forbade women from bathing their navels. Having melted the ice, I decided to bore him to death, then changed my mind.

"Father, would you give me an interview for my journal, *The Street*?"

"Yes, My Son, I can't refuse a lost lamb," he said.

I try to convince him that as a man I'm more like a ram than a lamb, but he'll have to read Alfred Pawels. No more man. No more awning. No more anything. Great. I suspect it must be the priest. Once he leaves they'll all return. Anyway, tough cookies—I begin my interview:

"Father, are you a Marxist?"

" No, My Son. Who's Marx?"

"A poor sinner, Father."

"Then pray for him, My Child."

He starts to pray.

Like a dope I fall under his influence and join my hands. But the snap of a brassiere strap nearby throws me back on track, and regaining my senses I continue:

"Father, do you f—?"

"No, My Son," he says. "What's that?"

"You don't f—?"

"No, My Son. I read my breviary."

"But the flesh?"

"Oh, it's good for nothing!"

I persist. "Are you an Existentialist, Father? Have you won the Plèiade Award?* Are you an anarcho-masochist, a Social-Democrat, a lawyer, a member of the Constituent Assembly of 1789, a wealthy land owner, or a black marketer in occult objects?"

"No, My Son, I pray and read *The Pilgrim* and sometimes *The Christian Witness*, but it's rather a liberal publication."

Undaunted, I continue: "Are you licensed to teach philosophy? Are you a marathon walker or champion of Basque soccer? Do you like Picasso? Do you give conferences in the religious sensibility of Rimbaud's work? Like Kierkegaard, are you one of those who believe that everything depends on the personal perspective of the individual? Have you published a critical text on *The hundred-and-twenty days of Sodom?*"

"No, My Son. I'm going on to Deligny where I live with the Lord's blessing. I repaint my church every two years and confess my parishioners," says the priest.

"But you'll never amount to anything, you silly fool!" I can't help saying, "Of all the— are you going to go on like this? You lead a ridiculous life. Not one worldly contact? No Cremona violin or Gericault trumpet? No hidden vice? Black Masses? Satanism?"

"No."

"Oh, Father, you're stretching the truth."

"I swear to you before God," he replies.

"But, Father, if you don't do any of the things I've mentioned do you realize that as a priest you don't exist?

"Alas, My Son," he says.

"Do you believe in God?"

"It goes without saying."

I tried my best to help. "Not even that?"

"I believe."

"You don't exist, Father. You simply don't exist. It can't be."

"It's true, My Son. You're right."

He looked crushed. I saw him blanch and his skin turned transparent. "What's come over you, Father? Don't worry. You still have time to write a book of poems."

"Too late," he mumbled; his voice came from far away. "What do you want? I believe in God and that's it."

"But such a priest doesn't exist," I mumbled in turn.

He became more and more evanescent and then evaporated into thin air. Damn, was I annoyed. No more priest.

As a souvenir, I took his breviary and each evening I read a bit from it. I found his address inside and from time to time I visit the little Presbytery where he lived. I'm an habitué. His maid consoled herself and really likes me now. Sometimes I confess the girls—the young ones—and drink the Communion wine. When all's said and done, it's not bad being a priest.

Reverend Boris Vian, N.S.C.J.
National Society of the Company of Jesus

* Vian's novel *L'ècume des jours*, Gallimard 1947, was nominated by Jean-Paul Sartre for the Prix de la Plèiade.

—*translated by Julia Older*

Bridget Meeds

The Salmon of Knowledge

Her father is outside, digging beneath the black walnut tree. He bails water; the earth is spring-wet, too full, winter melt weeping into the grave. Her mother is inside, wrapping the infant's body in a soft white blanket. The hole, meant for the placenta, will hold the whole child instead. At the memorial, the neighbor's small boy stares entranced at the full salmon on the table—the silver skin, the long delicate skeleton, the firm pink flesh. He touches the fish; his mother pulls back his hand. *You must wait until they stop speaking*, she whispers. He sucks his thumb, waiting. No seeds he has planted beneath the black walnut have ever grown, but he is too young to know why. This spring, he is trying again, in his secret way, with an apple pip.

Aimee Loiselle

The Things You Take, the Things You Leave

Eleanor wasn't surprised to find the door locked. Paul had changed all the locks five months earlier, when it became clear she wasn't going to stay at the house and she wasn't going to stay at rehab. She had left two programs, disappearing after she signed out of the second place. When she'd contacted Paul a couple weeks later, he told her that he'd hired a divorce lawyer. He said a year was too long to be dealing with this shit. Eleanor took the bus to their house so they could talk, but she had stayed for two nights. They'd drunk wine and had sex and cried and cooked pasta.

Standing on the porch with her backpack, Eleanor hoped Paul would let her in once he got home. She dropped her bag and looked around the front yard. Although the misty rain had stopped, the Seattle sky remained soft and gray. The hydrangeas she had planted three years ago were flush with round puffs of blue flowers, and the clematis had climbed far up the stick-and-twig trellis she'd built. But the large terra cotta pots where she used to plant cherry tomatoes sat empty. One was cracked and resting on its side.

Eleanor shaded her eyes and peered into the picture window. The living room was quiet, her plump tiger cat sprawled asleep on the couch. The sight of the relaxed cat suddenly made her feel both guilty and irrelevant. The cat's life went on without her. And Paul had replaced the two colorful throw pillows she'd bought at a craft fair in Olympia with smaller red and brown ones. Their wedding photo wasn't on the bookshelf anymore either, but she could see the familiar linen tablecloth in the dining room.

The stairs to the second floor were faded and dim through the window, but Eleanor recognized the general shape of a kimono Paul had hung on the wall. It was green, with intricate trees and long cranes embroidered in the bright silk. Eleanor turned and brushed off a chair before sitting down. She hoped the last of her clothes were still in the bedroom on the second floor. No matter what, she wanted to go through those as soon as she could.

Eleanor's desire to get into the house had taken hold after she woke up on the floor of an apartment that smelled like punky beer, sweat, and tomato sauce. A box from Lucia's Pizzeria sat on the kitchen counter next to an ashtray and a tall beer can. Inés, her sneakers tied tight and her head propped on a worn duffle bag, lay asleep in a ball behind Eleanor. Inés was also in her late thirties, but coils of gray had overtaken her curly black hair and hard lines were etched into the skin around her lips and eyes.

Eleanor wasn't able to find a clock. She stood, her thick brown hair falling around her pale face and onto her shoulders. She zipped her jeans, adjusted the long-sleeve t-shirt so it didn't pull across her chest, and slipped on her nylon rain jacket.

She recognized the basement apartment where she'd hung out the night before, and Kai was asleep in the ratty recliner. Eleanor felt comforted when she saw Kai, he was familiar. Like her, he had gone to college and enjoyed talking about city politics or museum exhibits. He read Edward Abbey and had a compliment for everybody—except people who played golf.

The square clock on the kitchen wall said a little after noon. Eleanor opened and closed her mouth, pushing her tongue against her fuzzy teeth. It only made matters worse. Now she could taste the film as well as feel it.

She wanted to shower. She wanted to shower in her own bathroom. In the clawfoot tub with the rust streaks around the drain. Eleanor imagined all the details—the white medicine cabinet, the yellow bath mat, the peppermint toothpaste. Although she didn't see herself in the room, she decided to go anyway.

The trick was Eleanor couldn't take Inés—she had grabbed the DVD player on their last visit and Paul said he'd call the cops if he saw Inés again. So Eleanor carefully lifted her black backpack and hugged it to her chest.

The man on the floor in front of Eleanor muttered and snuggled closer to the woman sleeping with him. They were both wearing flannel shirts over long-sleeved thermals, a common outfit in Seattle where the air cooled as soon as the sun went down. Eleanor moved lightly, stepping over them and clutching her backpack so it didn't hit anything. She reached the door, slowly turned the knob, and peered into the space at the bottom of the stairs. Across the hall, a stocky woman with a briefcase was locking the bolt on her door.

"Oh, ain't you a piece-a work," the woman snapped. "What are you mothafuckers doin' in there all night? Huh? You know, some of us have children. Some of us got to go to work." The woman stared past Eleanor into the apartment. "Look at all them crackheads up in there. God help me."

Eleanor winced. "Sorry," she whispered and shut the door behind her. "I'm not a crackhead. Really. I understand that you—"

"Dumbass white girl," the woman muttered. "It's the goddamn middle of the day." She wore dress pants, a silky blouse, and stylish leather boots, which she stomped up the stairs.

Eleanor waited at the bottom for the woman to leave and then started up. Halfway to the top, she heard Inés's voice. "Where the hell you goin? You said you was gonna stick round til we got in Fremont House."

Eleanor sighed. "Well I'm leaving, and I'm not going back in there."

"Alright, alright. Dios mío, you just had to wake me up. I can go."

Inés ducked back into the apartment for her things. For a second, Eleanor thought about taking off—running to hide in some entryway—but she'd told Inés that she would check the paperwork at Fremont House. The two women looked out for each other, and Eleanor was an expert at deciphering fine print. When she was at Pacific Northwest Legal Services, she'd worked with clients to file their paperwork. To challenge evictions or get restraining orders or fight for custody. She'd worked with them to make sure they weren't getting screwed, and their trust had given Eleanor a chance to feel real in the world.

The two of them stepped from the building. Inés had her duffle bag and a pack of cigarettes. She counted them as they walked to the corner.

"You only like menthol," Eleanor said.

"Yeah, but some pendejo left these on the table. There's eight cigarettes. I can sell em even if I don't smoke them."

"When did you say Fremont House will let you in?" Eleanor asked.

"You ain't stayin there?"

"No. I'm going home." Eleanor paused. "I gotta take a shower and get some of my stuff."

"Coño," Inés shook her head. "He ain't gonna let your ass back in that house. He already got lawyers and shit."

"That's why I gotta try. It's still my house," Eleanor said. The divorce papers weren't filed yet. Before she signed them, Eleanor wanted to see Paul.

"You gonna give up three weeks with a clean bed and a nice shared bathroom just because you want your own shower. Now who's the pendeja."

"I've got stuff there too." Eleanor stopped at the corner. "When can you get in?"

"Tomorrow. That's when they told me."

"Tomorrow?" Eleanor said. "Well. Let's go get a bottle." She looked around. "What do you wanna do? Go to the park?"

"We gotta go to the ramp first. I ain't got no money."

The ramp was an intersection off Interstate 5 where Inés and Eleanor first met. On her way home from Pacific Northwest Legal Services, Eleanor had sometimes driven past Inés and given her a few quarters. She'd also seen Inés around the neighborhood, outside the convenience stores or Chinese restaurants. The office was located in that area to be accessible to clients, and Eleanor often tracked them down if they missed appointments or court dates.

So when Eleanor spotted Inés arguing with a man at the end of the ramp, she'd grown concerned. Although the man stood facing traffic, he kept yelling over his shoulder at Inés. She was wearing terrycloth shorts and a grimy pink t-shirt with the word Kitty in glittering letters. When Eleanor reached to pass Inés the usual quarters, the man leapt for them and Eleanor had to pull her hand away as the light turned green. Listening to Inés cursing the man out in Spanish, Eleanor had turned the corner with the rest of the cars.

A week later, Eleanor had seen Inés walking into JJ's a few blocks from the PNLS office. Eleanor pulled over and checked to make sure she had a single dollar to give, and also noted that it was after five o'clock. The bar was dark except for an antique mirror that reflected a little sunlight from a small tinted window on the opposite wall. Inés was sitting alone and eyed Eleanor with suspicion when she said hello. Eleanor had to explain the incident at the ramp before Inés would invite her to pull up a stool. Eleanor ordered a glass of wine.

At the time, she still had her credit card and the two women drank until the bar closed nine hours later. Inés had told Eleanor that she was used to dealing with those pendejos who tried to force her off the ramp. Few women stayed on the street alone—women with babies went to shelters and most of the others found men. But not Inés. She said she hadn't had a man in two years, and at 38-years-old she didn't need one. The last man she'd hung out with had helped her stick needles in her arms and toes. He'd hustled with her. But she took care of herself now—she already had her tubes tied and three kids living in San Diego near their buela, so what did she need a man for?

Inés had also told Eleanor that she used to stay with men for money and company. She said men only hung around if you slept with them, which made the junkies easiest to live with. They didn't ask for as much pussy. But Inés had given all that up after her third court-ordered rehab, when she found out she was HIV negative. She thanked God and cried—she'd always figured she was positive so why bother stopping. Inés said once she was clean the men didn't seem so helpful, and their musty sex wasn't worth fighting over a few dollars. So she found her own money, bought her own drinks, and only smoked weed if she didn't have to fuck for it. She'd even started saving money for the bus ride to see her kids.

"Fine, let's go to the ramp," Eleanor said. She adjusted her back-pack and hit the pedestrian button on the light post. "I'm hungry though. I've got a little money left from the temp job. I can buy us a bottle, and some eggs and toast."

"You and your temp jobs," Inés laughed. "You think you the big lady cuz you got college. But look at you hangin out with una loca like me."

"We all have to work somehow, that's all."

"Pues, I think you're una loca. Cuz if I was you, I'd be goin to that house beggin that maricón to let me back in. I wouldn't give a shit what was wrong with him." Inés smiled. "Then once I was in, I'd come get you for a fancy dinner, and give you a big crystal glass with rum or champagne or whatever you wanted."

"I know, I know." Eleanor shrugged. "Maybe I'll feel like that when I get there."

After a couple hours at the ramp Inés had earned $12.74, so they each bought a fifth and walked to the park behind Pike Place Market. As soon as Inés joined a conversation, Eleanor wandered to a bench and took out her journal. It was just a spiral notebook, but she wrote in it every week like she had in college. An early fall breeze blew off Puget Sound and ruffled the pages against her pen.

That night, Eleanor and Inés followed a group of people from the park to a motel by the lumber port. Although Inés would have crashed on the floor again, Eleanor used the last of her money to get a separate room. When they joined the others, Eleanor took a seat on the beige and gray carpet next to a tall man named Martin who she often sat with in the park—she enjoyed his occasional comments about people in the market and the look of his calm face. She leaned against his shoulder, which smelled like cigarettes and exhaust. He called her Elly and shared his bottle of malt liquor. She passed him a cigarette whenever she smoked one.

Eleanor mentioned that she had a room and gestured toward the door with her head. They left and finished another bottle while Eleanor combed her fingers through Martin's tangled hair. He got up and went to the bathroom, which was quiet for a long time—she wondered if he had passed out or was taking a shit or just wanted to be alone. Then Eleanor heard the shower.

She fished through her backpack for the condoms, which she picked up whenever she passed the women's health center. It was the only place that had them out in a basket. She didn't know if the other women knew about it, so she always left extras in little piles on toilets or kitchen counters.

Martin came out of the bathroom with a dingy towel around his waist. "That felt good," he said. Eleanor was on the bed in her underwear and bra. "Elly. You got sweet eyes," he mumbled as he lay next to her. They kissed. The sex with Martin was close. He didn't pull away to look at her or hold her legs apart. He pressed his weight on her, and it was so private and serene she felt weepy. When they were done, he turned on the tv and watched a sitcom before dozing off. Eleanor slid her hand from his and went to take a shower.

The shower was better than nothing, but the motel didn't have soap or shampoo. The towels were gray and worn. She wanted a shower in her clawfoot tub, with honey-oatmeal soap and thick yellow towels the length of her whole body. She wanted to see Paul and decide if she needed to get the rest of her stuff. She didn't know if he would let her in this time, but she was going to try as soon as Inés got into Fremont House.

Martin had returned to the party by the time Eleanor stepped out of the bathroom, but she was relieved. She could get dressed in peace. After combing her hair and running a toothbrush over her teeth, she joined the others. The television was on. For the time being, everybody was happy and buzzed. A few men at the little round table were swapping stories, people were playing cards on the bed. Eleanor thought they were a beautiful mess.

She drank and smoked cigarettes till a guy dragged his girlfriend out the door and another one passed out by the tub and the booze was gone and the shabby carpet was littered with bottle caps and empty potato chip bags. With his mouth open and an empty bottle on his lap, Martin fell asleep against the wood paneling. So Eleanor and Inés decided to go back to their room as soon as Inés scanned for cigarettes, lighters, and other petty valuables.

Eleanor opened their shades wide before getting into bed. She wanted to wake up earlier than usual and get to Fremont House, but the light didn't burn through their stupor until after nine o'clock. The day was drizzly, which Eleanor hadn't mentally prepared for—Seattle usually remained clear and bright in September. Even after six years, Eleanor wasn't acclimated to the weeks of mist that came with the winter. When it had rained in Illinois, the rain came and went. Not in the northwest, although she could've handled the wet if she had more sun. Eleanor feared the months of gray cottony sky more than the rain. They buried her joy. Too many of those days and she felt desperate— she had to dip into her secret money, get herself a room, and find a temp job. If the temp agencies didn't have work, she would settle into the library for the stark fluorescent light and dazzling magazines.

When Eleanor and Inés reached Fremont House, Eleanor read the paperwork while the woman at the desk ran Inés's name to be sure she hadn't stayed at the shelter in the past year. "I told her I hadn't been here," Inés grumbled as they walked to the assigned room.

"Let's just get you set up. I gotta go," Eleanor said. "We got fifteen minutes before they kick me out."

"Yeah, yeah. I know. You gotta go to your house and ask your husband if you can take a shower. Yo sé, yo sé. But you ain't got no key and he ain't gonna let you in."

"We haven't signed the papers yet, I have a few more weeks. And he's gotta let me get my stuff if I want it."

"Hmph. Well you know about the law. Make sure you get your money from that house. And don't forget about me when you do. Remember the one that showed you where you could eat. Remember who looks out for you. Me oyes?"

Eleanor dropped her backpack onto the porch when she finally reached the house. She looked in at her sleeping cat and the throw pillows before dusting off a blue canvas chair. The air smelled spongy and green. She sat down, eventually dozing and waking to the scratchy sound of Paul's feet on the concrete steps.

"Eleanor," Paul sighed. "I can't take this right now. I've got a deadline on a Tokugawa paper. What do you want anyway?"

"I just want a shower," Eleanor said. Paul had his canvas messenger bag over his shoulder and a few student papers in one hand. She used to like watching him when he corrected their work, listening to some of the funny or illogical things they wrote.

"That's great. Let's all shuffle our lives around for your drinking and whenever you decide to take a shower." He slid his key in the bolt but didn't turn it. "We're reaching the end of this, you know that."

"Yes sir, I know that." Eleanor stood and threw her backpack over her shoulder. "I just wanna take a shower. This is still my house."

"Your name is on a piece of paper, that's all."

"Are you gonna be a jerk about this? I'm not really asking for anything difficult, and I haven't had a drink yet today."

Paul threw his head back. "Is that a joke?"

"No. I haven't had a drink yet, and it's after four o'clock."

"Wow. Well you better get started. You haven't had a drink in what, twelve hours? Your body might go into shock."

"You used to like my drinking. You used to drink with me."

"Not every day." Paul shook his head.

"Almost every day."

"Yeah, and I stopped doing that."

"Only when I started drinking every day. Because you were afraid to admit it, you drank a little less." Eleanor smiled. "That's not really stopping."

"Shut up," he said and unlocked the door.

Eleanor followed him into the house. "I can have a drink right? You're not going to block me from the cabinet, you haven't moved the liquor."

"What's the point? You'd just find a way to sneak it."

"Not anymore. I only drink in the open now."

"Good for you. That's quite a step." Paul left his bag on a chair in the dining room. "Where's Inés? Too busy for a visit this time?"

Eleanor ignored him and poured a glass of scotch. She sat on the couch with the cat, who purred and rolled against her leg. Paul opened the refrigerator. "I'm hungry, so I hope you don't mind, but I've gotta eat something."

"No, I don't wanna get in the way," Eleanor answered. "Would it be alright if I ate here? I'd really like to stay, at least till I find another job."

"Oh yes, the temp jobs."

"Don't look down your fucking nose. You're such a hypocritical bastard—Mister Progressive who supports the janitors' right to a living wage. But you can't stand that your wife works as a temp filing papers. The kinda work that makes your research possible by the way."

"You have a bachelor's degree and a paralegal certificate, Eleanor." Paul appeared in the doorway. "You were going to apply to law school. What the fuck do you want me to say?"

"That you're happy I found a way to be happy with what I've got."

"I don't think you're really happy. And I'm not gonna listen to that shit about how we all die anyway so why bother."

"You just can't take the truth. I mean, you think your work on obscure Japanese emperors is going to make you immortal. That's really why you do it. And who says that's so important?"

"I told you I'm not listening to that shit. But at least I'm doing something productive."

"Yeah." Eleanor finished her drink. "So can I take a shower now?"

"You know where it is," Paul gestured toward the stairs.

Eleanor set her backpack on the bed in the guestroom and stripped naked. It was a delight. She was naked, and nobody was waiting for the shower or the toilet. It was a luxury. She strolled to the bathroom and closed the door. The hot water ran over her from head to toe as steam filled the room. She waited until every part of her body was soaked before reaching for the shampoo. It smelled like rosemary. The body scrub was citrus.

The water stayed hot as Eleanor washed every inch of her skin with the honey-oatmeal soap. The whole bathroom was a warm haze. She turned the cold water down and stood with the heat falling on her neck and back. After her muscles completely relaxed, Eleanor turned off the water. Tears pushed at the back of her eyes. She wasn't going to come here anymore.

Eleanor wrapped the towel around her head and walked to the guestroom. Her backpack was on its side. And the zipper wasn't closed all the way. She studied it, wondering what Paul had touched, if he'd taken anything. The condoms were still in the side pocket, but that didn't mean he hadn't seen them. Even though she was irritated, she decided not to say anything. She wanted to have a decent dinner with him. She wanted a final memory of the whole thing.

Eleanor emptied the backpack on the bed and made three piles—things to throw out, things to wash, things to pack immediately. When she turned around, Paul was standing at the door. He was watching her. "You look thin," he said. "You lost weight."

Eleanor felt exposed and her nakedness became terrible. She tilted her head, spun the towel from her hair, and wrapped it around herself.

"I've seen you naked before." Paul smiled and took a sip of his red wine. It was in a large water glass, almost empty. "What's with the shyness?"

"It's all different … you know things are different now. We're not really … I'm just gonna do some laundry and that's it. Then we can have dinner."

Paul didn't move from the doorway.

Eleanor planted her feet and crossed her arms. "Are you gonna let me get my stuff? Or do we have to get in a fight first."

Paul didn't move. "Why are you doin' this Eleanor? Why are you just gonna piss everything away?"

"That again, come on Paul. What everything?" Eleanor exhaled. "The same words in different order."

"You say that, but you keep coming back. How many times has it been?"

Eleanor glanced around the bedroom before looking right at Paul. "Not this time, this is it. I've never said it this way before."

"You're not coming back because I changed the locks and we're getting a divorce and you won't have this house anymore. That's why you're not coming back."

"I just want the rest of my stuff." Eleanor tried to shove past him, but he held his arm out against her, knocking her back on her heels. "You're a pathetic asshole."

"Don't push me Eleanor," he said.

Fear squirmed through Eleanor's belly. She knew when Paul drank he felt comfortable forcing his demands. He yelled and grabbed and threw things, excusing himself as passionate. She knew he wanted her to stay in their marriage, but she wasn't going to.

"Let me by," she demanded.

"No, you're gonna listen—"

Thinking she needed to make a point, Eleanor slapped him across his face. A little wine spilled on the hardwood floor. "Don't you fucking tell me what to do in my own house," she said. "Don't threaten me. I put money and work into this house. I paid my fucking bills and did what—"

Paul grabbed the back of her neck and pushed the glass of wine to her mouth. "Here. Here's what you want." The glass hit Eleanor's teeth and wine ran down her clean chin and neck. She sputtered, sprinkling Paul's t-shirt with the wine. "Goddamn you bitch."

"What'd you do, swig a bottle of wine while I was taking a shower? You drink it," she yelled. "You're nothing but a fucking drunk, you just pretend you're not."

Paul took Eleanor's arm and whipped her down the short hall into the master bedroom. Her towel almost fell. "Here, get your clothes. That's all you want. That's all you came for. Then get out." He set the glass down and pressed his forehead against the edge of the dresser.

Eleanor held the towel to her chest and used the corner to wipe the wine from her face. She opened her dresser drawers. They were already half-empty, but she scooped up the last of her socks and underwear and walked to the guestroom, where she stuffed them in her backpack. Returning to the bedroom, she stepped into the closet to get her work and dress clothes. She planned to walk out of the house in $120 Anne Taylor pants and a $250 cashmere sweater. That was it.

Paul followed her. His breath, which smelled like scotch and wine, filled the tight area. "I'm sorry, I didn't mean . . ." He put his arms around Eleanor and spoke into the back of her head. "I just don't know what to do. I'm lost here."

Eleanor stood still. She knew this strategy too—when Paul realized he'd pushed too hard and came looking for pity. She stared at the dark ceiling. "Don't grab me like that anymore, Paul. We're both upset, but I don't deserve that shit."

"I love you Eleanor. I want to work this out, I want to help you get sober."

"I don't want to be sober. I'm not interested in it."

"You're not interested in this marriage either?"

"Not anymore."

Paul pressed his lips to her hair. Eleanor held off the cringe that threatened to curl her spine. "I just can't believe it," he said. "We've been together since college, we've been through everything." He pressed his body against her.

She felt his expectation. It pushed against the top of her right butt cheek. She felt no fondness or excitement, but she wanted to pack her clothes and do laundry and have something to eat. "Fine. Paul. If this is what you want. Let's go," she jerked herself around and faced him. "Let's get it over with."

"What do you mean?"

"You know what I mean."

"Eleanor, don't make this . . . it's that I love you. Can't you see?"

Eleanor stepped from the closet and dropped the towel. She held out her arms. "Let's go Paul. If this is what you have to have."

He followed her from the closet and picked up the towel. He wrapped it around her, hugging her and pressing her to his chest. His dick, with all its persistence, rubbed on her hip. He kissed her forehead and her cheek, but Eleanor turned her face away. "I just don't want . . . you've been a part of my life for almost fifteen years," he muttered. He didn't try to kiss her mouth. "I need you."

She dropped onto the bed. Paul lay next to her with one leg over hers. He ran his hand along her stomach and breasts and hips, and she lay quiet.

"I've missed you," he whispered. "I can't believe that . . . you're really leaving."

She waited. She didn't move a muscle. She waited. She prayed and wished that he wouldn't do it.

Paul unzipped his pants and wriggled out of them. He crawled on top of her, directing himself into her. He made muffled questioning noises until he was all the way in. Then he groaned. Eleanor didn't move.

He rocked back and forth and grabbed under her back. He buried his face in her hair for a couple minutes. Then he rose on his arms and looked down at where their bodies met. He studied himself moving in and out before falling on his elbows and closing his eyes. He jammed harder against her pelvis, arched his back, and finished.

After resting on top of her, he shifted away and distractedly ran a hand along her arm. He sighed. "You know . . . I love you," he mumbled.

Eleanor waited. She listened for his breathing to get raspy.

She went to the bathroom and sat on the toilet while Paul's sex dripped out of her. She only felt free of it after three handfuls of toilet paper.

"What're you doin'?" Paul muttered.

"I wanna get a load of laundry in," Eleanor whispered. "Shhh, go back to sleep."

She took another shower, but it was quick. She barely noticed the water. She hurried to the guestroom and put on her black pants, burgundy cashmere sweater, Prada boots, and a pair of platinum hoop earrings.

The sky was growing dim. Eleanor needed to get going. She grabbed all the soap, shampoo, and conditioner and crammed them in the backpack with her clothes. When the backpack was full, she went to the corner room and got Paul's large frame pack and his sleeping bag. She used his backpack for shoes, boots, toenail clippers, barrettes, deodorant, and toothpaste. She snuck into the bedroom. Paul was snoring. She took his shaving kit and loaded it with her remaining jewelry, his wedding band, his Tag Heuer watch, both mini-reading lights, and all the change from the mug in his top drawer.

She carried both packs downstairs and took bags of ham and cheese and a container of Hunan chicken from the refrigerator. She put them in a paper bag with four apples and a grapefruit. She didn't know how she'd carry it all, but she wedged the vodka and rum into Paul's backpack anyway. When she finished, Eleanor poured a glass of scotch and sat on the couch. The house grew shadowy. The diffused sunlight, filtered through layers of clouds, fell below the trees. A slate glow reflected off Lake Washington.

Eleanor finished her drink but still didn't know where to stay for the night. She needed money. So she crept up the stairs and fished through Paul's pants for his wallet. He had $67. She could get a room for the night. In the morning, she'd sell the watch and some jewelry and that would give her enough to keep the room for a week and find a temp job.

The cat yawned and stretched on the couch as Eleanor tied the packs closed, checking to make sure all the clips were snapped as Inés had advised her. Eleanor bent to kiss the cat and cried. She slid to her knees and cried that she couldn't take the cat. Cried that their choices meant Paul got the cat. Eleanor wanted her. But she wanted other things.

Eleanor loaded Paul's backpack onto her shoulders. She slid her own pack over her chest. The sleeping bag went in one hand, the paper bag in the other. She stepped out the front door and glanced at the clematis and hydrangeas, the trillium and Japanese maple. She'd liked her garden.

It was eight o'clock at night, but before going to JJ's, Eleanor had to get a room, a private room for sleeping and washing before work. Not for parties. She walked to the nearest bus stop because the best nightly rooms were at the edge of downtown. By the time she filled out the paperwork and got her key, the digital clock bolted to the table said 9:54. Eleanor dropped the bags and stretched her fingers. She peeked in the bathroom. The shower was a fiberglass stall with mildew around the rubber pads on the floor. Eleanor sat on the bed and pulled Paul's backpack to her lap. She found the bottle of vodka and took a drink. It seared her throat just right. She took another drink.

By the time she reached JJ's, Inés and another regular named Janice were already drunk, laughing with a skinny man in a short-sleeved oxford and an ugly red tie. Three twenties and a ten dollar bill were set under his beer glass, next to a pack of Marlboro reds.

Janice laughed and threw out her hands when she saw Eleanor. "Hey, look at Miss Princess."

Eleanor shrugged and smiled. She knew she looked absurd.

"Ay cabrona," Inés said. "I told you he wouldn't let you stay with him no more, but you got your stuff. That's good. Qué guapa, blanquita."

"Well hello," the skinny man said. "My name is Drew." He held out a hand.

Eleanor shook it. "I'm Eleanor."

"What're ya drinkin Eleanor?"

Janice leaned over the bar. "Look at her clothes. She can buy her own fuckin drink."

"I'd like to buy the lady a drink," Drew said. "No need to get greedy, I got plenty-a money."

"I'll take a Stoli," Eleanor said and sat next to Drew, on the other side from Inés and Janice. Inés laughed and shook a cigarette from Drew's pack. Eleanor got one from her own, and Drew lit both cigarettes with the Zippo he flicked open.

"Gracias," Inés nodded.

Eleanor didn't say anything.

"Don't ya say thank you when a gentleman lights your cigarette?" Drew asked.

"No," Eleanor answered. She stared at him. He shrugged. The vodka came and Eleanor sipped it. She knew what type of guy he was. A working guy who didn't make enough money to keep a girlfriend but made enough to get laid by the drunks at the dive bar.

When the bartender turned on the lights and yelled for everybody to leave, Eleanor pocketed her cigarettes and walked out with Inés, Janice, and Drew. "We're goin to Drew's house," Inés said. "His brother is there with a bagga weed."

"That's okay," Eleanor said. "I think I'm gonna take off."

"You goin back to your ex's place?" Inés asked.

"No," Eleanor shook her head. "I got somewhere to stay. What're you gonna do? You missed curfew."

"I got two nights I can miss," Inés said with a wink. "It takes a while to get used to all those rules."

"Well, well. Elly must got herself a mystery man," Janice said with a playful smirk.

"No," Inés smiled. "Not mi amiga de piedra. She don't do that kinda shit."

Eleanor walked to a secret bar that stayed open until three in the morning in the tiny basement of a gay club. It was decorated with velvet and gold trim, like a 19th-century brothel. She ordered bottom-shelf vodka and smoked cigarettes. The guy next to her was talking to the bartender about a new movie he'd seen that night. Eleanor listened as she watched the crowd, but the lights came up before she found someone she knew. People climbed the stairs to the alley and scattered into the darkness, disappearing around corners or into cars. The moon was a hazy sliver through the clouds. Eleanor lifted her arms to the night sky before lighting a cigarette and heading toward her building.

Carrie Shipers

DISCARDS
—after Albert Goldbarth

This book is a tribute to a famous man I once fucked
in the stacks of an equally famous library. It took

seven years to write. The sex scenes are disappointing.
This cookbook requires ingredients from expensive

gourmet stores—pomegranate syrup, artichoke hearts
harvested in utter silence. This book was made possible

by large grants from corporations that make me sick.
I suspect they're poisoning my groundwater. I rescued

this book from a men's room. I wanted to preserve it
as a cultural artifact but found the responsibility too great.

I stole this book from a friend who didn't admire it
enough. I swore we'd be together forever

but have since lost interest. This book is like new
except for the cigarette burns and chocolate ice cream.

It reeks of tequila and has already been replaced
by a similar book that is still a virgin. Dripping gore

and good intentions, this book should not be left alone
with children. This book was the last book I bought before

I stopped buying books. Every day it taunts me.
This book has been asked to leave other libraries.

Yu Xiang

2002, I Have

I have a door on which it's written:
Warning: You may become lost!

I have several pieces of paper, the kind without lines
that records my shameless verse
and I don't know where the good times have gone.
Instead I'm left with a shriveled wallet and a bit of talent.

If I were an obedient girl,
I would be a good daughter, good citizen, good lover. I would
chuck my freedom out the window and never write another
    poem.

But I'm a disgusting person
with dirty feet and discount scarf
that make my man a real man,

make him happy, brave, suddenly in love with life.
I have a real man. I have
arms I use to embrace. I have
a right hand I use to squeeze, to throw things, to shake hands
    with strangers.
I have a left hand I use to caress and love,

yet where did those painful affairs go?
Those entanglements, extra key rings.
I have cigarettes to blacken my lungs, yellow
my fingers. I have the light of self-knowledge.
I have passion and I have wounds. I have

electricity. You'd be happy if it sets you on fire.
I have a place to hide and a P.O. Box. I have
birth control pills and sleeping pills. I have
a phone, red like lust. I have
a habit of dialing numbers. I have heard
enough of its rings. Why do I always call
places where no one picks up?

—translated by Joanna Sit and Keming Liu

Teacher of Athletes

I never seen J. J. Packard fight till the day my father picked up the Jersey City *Eagle* and did a little jig in front of East's Cigar Store on the corner of Spain Street and Buckeye.

"Hot damn," he said. The newspaper rattled like dead leaves in a hurricane, and the pages scattered on the ground while he danced.

"Hot damn," he said again, "J. J. Packard is fighting downtown today. He must remember me. We were like that. Shit." He lowered the paper and looked at me. He looked at me like I was somebody else's kid or maybe I wasn't even there. I was used to that, and I didn't say anything. He didn't want me to. He talked at me just because I was there, and he talked to himself when I wasn't. I seen him do it before.

My father picked up the pages on the ground and started folding the paper back the way it was. Then he folded it again, and tucked it under his arm. When he lifted his arm, I could smell the sweat and I tried not to show it. My father knew about his smell and he didn't like to hear about it. If you showed him you knew it, he might slap the shit out of you right there on the sidewalk for reminding him. He started walking down Spain Street toward downtown, and as I began to follow, there was a yell behind us.

"Ain't you gonna pay for it, Mac?" The counterman was standing by the newspaper rack.

"Yeah," said my father, "I'm gonna pay for it." He dug a coin out of his pocket and tossed it to the guy. "See, I'm payin' for it." He walked off down the street again. The guy looked at the coin and shook his head.

By then I knew we was both going to the fights, and I ran to catch up with my father. I was happy and I wasn't watching, so when my father whistled I was surprised. The street was noisy, but my father could always make a wolf-whistle louder than the traffic whenever he saw some babe. I looked up when he whistled and I seen her walking up the street towards us. She just swished right by him without even looking. I walked closer to the shop windows like I was looking in, so nobody would think I was with him. I watched him in the reflection so I didn't lose him, like I did a couple of times before when he started walking in a hurry all of the sudden.

In the glass, I saw my father look up and yell at somebody across the street. The guy started running and my father ran after him. The soles of his shoes whacked the pavement loud where they was coming loose, and I ran too to see what was up. They both ran around a corner, and when I got there, they was gone, but I kept running up to the next alley and found them. My father had his arm across the guy's throat up against the wall. The guy's feet kicked against the bricks like he was nailed up there. Then I knew who he was. It was this guy Sollie that my father met when we first got to Jersey City and was staying downtown, before we moved to the park at night. My father was searching Sollie's pockets while he twitched and hissed and cursed.

"Shut your damn yap, Sollie," my father hissed back. "Can't you see my kid's here? Don't want to spoil him, do ya?"

Sollie hissed something else, but my father leaned harder on his throat and he gagged. From where I stood down the alley, it looked like two guys kissing and pawing each other.

"Hello," says my father. "What the hell is this?" He pulled a wad of crumpled green from Sollie's pants. "You son of a bitch."

My father let Sollie slide to the ground while he counted out some of the bills. He counted them again, then took three more, and threw the rest in the mud where Sollie was rubbing his throat and choking.

"Don't double-cross me, Sollie. It's expensive. I got your number, you little bastard." My father kicked at his stomach, but Sollie rolled away and reached the rest of the bills after him. My father walked up the alley back to the street.

"C'mon, kid. We're goin' to the fights. You're gonna see a real fighter tonight, not some palooka who thinks a five of clubs is part of a poker hand. J. J. Packard is some mean son of a bitch."

J. J. Packard was his name. Or at least that's the way promoters billed him, over his other title, "The Good White Hope." The insiders said he hated his first name but kept the initial to make himself mad without having to see it. Nobody argued with a man like Packard. He took offense real quick, and always paid back in deuces any chump who double-crossed him. That's what the insiders said. He never talked much around reporters, and they didn't like him much. He talked to the guys in the second floor gym where he trained and fought, though. I found that out later when I asked for myself. All the insiders had a different story about Packard. It was funny, because they all seen the same thing but told it different. Only thing I never figured out was why they only called him "The Good White Hope."

We came out of the alley and started walking downtown again. I felt fine. I liked going to the fights. I liked the noise, and the smells of the sweat of the fighters, and the blue cloud of smoke, and the perfumed and powdered babes who get hot at the fights.

I guess it was lucky my father seen Sollie across the street. I was pretty sure we was low on money, since my father wasn't working right then. Most times my father would sell things wherever we was. He was a good salesman. One guy said one time that my father always sold himself to the marks first, and if they bought that, they'd buy whatever else he was selling. Even when my father was alone, he talked to himself to keep himself company. I guess he didn't seem alone then, and I seen him plenty of times talking to himself when he was getting better that time we lived in K.C., when I lifted papers to sell for food. He would read the paper out loud and yell at it sometimes. That's what he was like. He was like a lot of people all at once.

We got to the gym through the alley door and climbed the stairs. When we got inside, my father slipped down through the crowd and got us some seats ringside. We was in the second row. The challenger's corner was on the left, but I couldn't see the other corner from where I was sitting, since I was still short in those days.

My father handed me the newspaper from under his arm and stood up to look in the other corner. I tried to hold the newspaper away from me without my father seeing. The newspaper was soggy on the advertisement for the fight we was seeing. It was the first time I seen the name of the guy Packard was gonna fight. Some palooka name of André Christenson. I never heard of him before, and I never heard of him after that fight neither. The date was right over Packard's name. June 28, 1920. I remember that, because after the fight I decided to make it my birthday. My father told me I was born in June, but he couldn't remember what the day really was, and I figured it wouldn't matter anyway.

The house lights went down and a fat guy in a black suit stepped into the ring and started waving his hands for quiet.

"Ladies and gentlemen," he yelled.

I didn't hear any of the rest of it, because my father leaned across me to talk to some dame who was sitting on the other side in front of me. I held my breath for as long as I could, then leaned my head back to get some air. The guy behind me looked at me and reached over to tap my father on the shoulder.

"Something's wrong with the kid."

My father turned his head to look at me over his shoulder.

"He's all right. Just every once in awhile he gets these spells. First time was on a train from St. Louis." I held my breath while he told a story. My father did that a lot. It was a long one, and I'd heard parts of it before. I musta been pretty blue by the time I heard the bell. There was black spots in my eyes, but I could see the two fighters circling each other in the ring. Christenson was blocking my view at first, but then he stepped to the side and I seen Packard.

J. J. Packard was a bull in the ring, huge and hairy, with black hair all over his chest and back. His hair was cut short and laid down real close to his head. He had a mustache, and he was smiling. He circled around Christenson, and you could see that it was gonna be a slaughter. Packard was dipping and weaving around, and Christenson was walking almost flat-footed, circling in a kinda crouch around his gloves. Packard stood up straight, and the lines of his body was so clean it made you feel like somebody just cut him out of a boulder. It made my throat ache just to see it, like those statues I seen somewhere when

I was real little. He looked like a fighter oughta look. He was big and hard, and his eyes got real bright just before he took the first swing.

Christenson seen it coming and ducked it. He counter-punched, one, two, to the gut. Packard came right in over it and hit him right in the pan. It sounded like a door slamming. Christenson sagged a little more each time they came out of a clinch. The round was just about over when Christenson surprised Packard with a fast bunch of punches. One was an upper-cut that connected with Packard's jaw. He staggered to a stand, and Christenson was all over him. Packard hid his face and backed up till he felt the ropes behind him, then threw a punch out that split Christenson's eyebrow open. Blood spurted and got in his eye, so he kept trying to wipe it out, and Packard was socking him a punch at a time to the other side of the ring when the bell rang. Christenson backed over to the corner and fell on the stool. His trainers was all around him, giving him advice and rubbing him down, but he was still dazed from Packard's last volley. One of the trainers took out some tape and stuck it over Christenson's eyebrow and wiped the blood out. Then the trainers all climbed out through the ropes and the bell rang.

Christenson stood and walked to the middle of the ring. Packard was already waiting for him. He jabbed right between Christenson's gloves, and Christenson's head snapped back. His sweat made a mist in the air under the hot lights, and Packard's glove darkened with the wet. He worked Christenson over to the ropes and hooked a left to the side of Christenson's head, and as the referee was crossing behind him to see, he dropped a right, low in the gut, that brought the whole place to its feet, screaming.

Everybody was standing all around me, and I couldn't see what the yelling was about, but most people thought Christenson was fouled. My father and a guy next to him was yelling at each other about it. My father was saying Packard hadn't fouled anybody. Anybody who wasn't blind could see that. The other guy was yelling back, but I couldn't make it out. By the time everybody sat down again, the bell ended the second round.

Christenson was already in his corner when I could see again, and he was bent over, holding his stomach. He was shaking pretty bad, and

I think one of the trainers was trying to convince him to stop the fight. The other one was on one knee, talking to Christenson as he wiped his face and rubbed his side. Then both of them climbed through the ropes again, and the bell rang.

Packard was already dancing in the middle of the ring before Christenson even stood up, and one of Christenson's trainers put a hand through the ropes and pushed him. Christenson slapped at the hand and stood up. He got his stance and walked toward Packard. The insiders all say Packard was always big on opening right up. He jabbed hard, right at Christenson's face as soon as he was close enough. Christenson blocked it and caught Packard solid on the jaw, then followed with two quick body blows that made Packard's skin red under the curly black hair. Packard shook his head and brought up a roundhouse that connected solid with Christenson's jaw, and there was a snap I heard even over the yelling of my father next to me. Christenson covered his face and Packard beat at his belly real mad, backing him up to the ropes right above us. Then he leaned back just before Christenson got to the ropes and landed a real hard gut punch. Christenson folded, backing through the ropes, and fell out onto the guys in front of us. They seen him coming down and reached up to save themselves or catch him, but he was so heavy they both collapsed under his weight, and after they broke most of his fall, he came down on me and my father. He landed mostly on my father, who went down under him, and Christenson's head landed in my lap as I fell back.

His face was covered with blood and sweat, and he was choking, so I reached his mouthpiece out. Blood gushed out and ran down his cheeks and into my lap and on my shirt. He was trying to talk. I leaned over him.

"Kid. Save me, kid," he mumbled, trying to smile.

It was awful, and I sat up. The blood and sweat was making my clothes soggy, and my crotch was getting wet. I felt sorta sick, like when I had to wear one of my father's shirts and I couldn't get away from the smell.

Christenson started to mumble again, but I didn't get it. There was a big commotion as my father crawled out from under the big fighter. He was cursing a blue streak and getting out of the way of the trainers dragging Christenson out of my lap.

"C'mon Mac, move it, will ya?" said one of the trainers. He was trying to get his arm under Christenson's back and shoulder to lift him off me.

The two trainers got Christenson on his feet, stretched his arms across their shoulders, and carried him down the aisle with his feet dragging and blood running down his chest.

I looked up, and Packard was leaning over the ropes, one glove reached out toward Christenson. Sweat and blood was dripping off him, but he was smiling and yelling as Christenson's trainers dragged him away.

"André. C'mon André. We got to keep ourselves amused, don't we? C'mon back!"

My father climbed over the seats in front of us to where Packard was standing. He yelled up at him, but Packard didn't hear him at first. Then Packard looked down and saw him. He smiled. They yelled to each other, but I still couldn't hear them. Packard stooped down and started talking with my father. They talked fast, and once my father pointed back at me, and Packard glanced at me. The bright eyes narrowed for a second, then he looked at my father again. People was climbing through the ropes, and the fat guy in the black suit was grabbing at Packard's arm to hold it over his head. Packard slapped my father on the shoulder lightly and nodded while he stood up again. The crowd surrounded him and he was gone, and I could hear the fat guy yelling, but no one was listening. My father climbed back over the seats to me.

"C'mon. Let's get out of here."

He wasn't looking at me and probably didn't know if I was following him or not when he walked away.

Outside, my father stopped and bought a cigar. He stuck it in his pocket.

"It's gettin' late," said my father. "Go on over to the park, and I'll see ya there later. I got some business."

He walked off downtown, and I went to the park. It was three streets over, and I found the same old bench with the thick green paint empty in the streetlight when I got there. I washed Christenson's blood off me in the fountain, and then I sat down and pulled my cap over my eyes and crossed my arms. Right off, I started thinking about Packard. Now, that guy was a fighter. My father was right about him. I kept hearing that slam to the face and seeing the mist in the air, and the little way Packard smiled and stepped back to admire his work when he landed one. I remember thinking I wanted to be a fighter like Packard myself, and I tried to figure out how a guy might do it. I musta fell asleep, because I was dreaming Packard and me was on a train crossing a bridge over a big river. The next I knew, my father was kicking at my foot with his toe.

"Hey, kid. C'mon." I pushed my cap up and looked at him. The sun was rising over his left shoulder, and I had to squint. I stood up and rolled my shoulders, ticking my tongue in my mouth. He was already walking off. I ran to catch up.

We musta walked all over that town that day. We went all over the place and I never did figure out why. I never asked, and he never told me. He left me standing in the street while he went in places, but it was never too long. It was about quitting time for working guys when my father came out of the last building we went to that day. He didn't look at me.

"Let's eat," he said.

We crossed the street and walked into a little lunchroom called Max and Al's. There was a long counter with a clock over it and a long mirror on the wall. My father looked at it and then turned down the row of booths next to the big front window. He stopped at the second booth and slid in. I walked to the other side and slid in. From where I was sitting, I could see the waitress behind the counter with her elbow on it, drinking some coffee while she watched us. When she was sure we wasn't gonna get up again, she picked up two menus and walked over to us. She put one in front of my father and the other one in front of me. I didn't pick mine up. My father was already talking to the waitress.

"Is there a special today?" My father looked at her. "You look pretty special to me."

"Order from the menu, Mac."

I stared at the menu laying on the table in front of me.

"Yeah, well, bring me a roast beef Manhattan with mashed potatoes and gravy and an extra roll. Give the kid a bowl of the soup *du jour* of the day."

"Is that all you want, kid?" she said.

"Bring us both some coffee, too," said my father. "We had a big breakfast on the train this morning."

She looked back at my father, tilting her head to the side.

"Right," she said.

Behind me, a guy leaned over the back of the seat.

"Hey, did you say you just got in on the train?"

"Sure did," said my father. "Just got in from Chicago."

"Hey, now that's the way to travel. I been hitching rides all up and down the coast for my new job lately. It's hell to have to hitch around selling things."

"What're you selling?"

"Shoes. That's what I'm selling. I wore out plenty of 'em sellin' 'em, too. See?"

He held his foot out in the aisle for my father to see.

"I sell 'em for a friend of mine. I been needing a job and it just so happened I knew this guy when we was kids, and I walked in and said, 'John, you remember back when we was kids in West Virginia, and I used to look out for you? Well, now I need some looking after.' He said it was a pretty good pitch for a job and hired me right then and there. I been hitching around trying to open up some new markets for his shoes. Been doing pretty good, too. Always carry a bunch of 'em in this case," he said, patting something under the table.

"No chance you need some shoes now, is there? These shoes guaranteed to last a solid year. I know. I been walking around in mine that long. Can't say I ain't walked a mile in *these* shoes," he laughed.

My father laughed too.

The waitress brought the food then, and I picked up my spoon and stopped listening. I was really hungry. I stopped listening because I knew I'd hear that guy's story again, and pretty soon I'd get it by heart, and the first time's not that interesting if you're going to know it by heart. See, my father used to talk to people and hear them tell stories and then he'd tell them later, like maybe they was about a friend of his, or his brother did it, and then later he'd tell the story, and by that time it had happened to him. He always added stuff that really did happen to him, but he stuck that in the stories from the other people. I asked him about it once and he walloped me, just like when I told him his sweat stunk. I never asked him about it again, and he kept right on doing it. My father was putting down his knife when I looked up. He scooped the last two bites of the Manhattan up on his fork and into his mouth. He already ate everything else except for the extra roll. He took one bite out and set it down.

"Be seein' ya, Paul," my father said as he stood up.

The guy behind us waved and kept on chewing. When my father turned around to walk up to the till, I reached the roll into my pocket. I got up and walked over to where he was paying. He was talking to the waitress who was getting his change.

"It's a beautiful town," he said, "with lots of beautiful sights."

"Yeah," said the waitress closing the drawer and dropping the change in his hand, "one."

She turned and walked toward her coffee cup, down the counter aisle. The wicket to the kitchen came up as she went by, and some food on white plates slid out. She stopped and started loading it on her arms. My father stopped watching and pushed the door open and went out. I followed him. He was standing on the sidewalk lighting a cigar.

"We're going to see J. J. Packard," my father said.

It was a long walk and it was cooling off a little, but my father was still sweating and we was walking pretty slow. I moved over to the other side by making out I seen a coin on the sidewalk, then faking a miff when it wasn't. I kicked a stone into the street and walked on the other side. There was shadows in the street by the time my father stopped walking. He looked up at the brick front of the building.

"This is it. Mrs. Bell's Rooming House."

He knocked on the door at the top of the steps. A fat lady in a green dress with a white apron opened the door and came out.

"Is J. J. Packard here?"

"You wanna see him?"

"Yeah, if he's here."

She looked at him a minute and then looked at me.

"This your son? He's a handsome jack. Looks like he got a touch of the tar brush though," she said with a sly squint at my father's face. My father started to tell her the story about me. The story was about how my mother was a full-blooded Cherokee Indian he met when he was a traveling salesman. He settled down for a snowbound winter in a teepee on the plains with her, and something beautiful happened, and I was born the next June. He didn't know the day, but that was all right because I didn't believe any of it anyway. Every time I snitched the Eagle, there was another story about somebody's mother or grand-mother or great-grandmother being some Indian or another. Funny, nobody ever claimed an Indian father or grandfather or great-grandfather, but it didn't matter anyway. I figured I was dark because it was June and my father and I didn't have any place to go, since he wasn't working.

Mrs. Bell led us up a flight of stairs, down a hall, up more stairs, down another hallway, and then down another hall, while my father told the story of me and my mother's death.

"So that winter she chewed rawhide all the time. Chewed rawhide right in her teeth, and pretty white teeth they were," my father was saying.

"Here's his room," said Mrs. Bell.

My father drew himself up on the worn heels of his shoes.

"Thank you, Mrs. Bell. Thank you very much. It is *Mrs.* Bell, ain't it?"

"Oh, yeah, I'm Mrs. Bell, all right. And I shore would like to know where Mr. Bell is by a damn sight."

"Foolish man to leave a flower like you behind," my father said. I leaned against the wall with my hands in my pockets and my head down. The door to Packard's room opened and he stuck his head out.

"I thought that was you hustling out here in the hall, Joe. Come on in, and bring the kid." He didn't say anything to Mrs. Bell but she hurried down another hallway anyway.

We went into the room. There was no lights in the room and it was pretty dark outside the window, so I stepped to the side and stood waiting till I could see better.

"Is it okay?" said my father from the darkness in the middle of the room. "You said come by late. Sure looks like everybody is gone all right."

"Yeah, Joe, you're okay," Packard said, closing the door behind me.

The wood rubbed at the top corner and he thumped it shut with his fist.

"Here, let me get some light in this place."

I closed my eyes and opened them again, and a lamp was lit on the wall. I could see now that the room was small, with two chairs and a desk over by the window, and a table in the corner by the door. Some newspapers was folded up on the table, but they was rumpled like they been opened a couple of times.

J. J. Packard had his back to me, and when he turned around, he seemed even bigger than he was in the ring. He looked at me, and then at my father, and smiled. His smile was real wide, with a lot of teeth and a real skinny nose he said never got broke, but the insiders told me later they wasn't sure about that. I couldn't see his eyes, but they looked dark.

He walked over, picked up a chair, and set it by my father. My father sat down and Packard hitched a leg over the chair by the table, reaching himself a bottle from the other side of the newspaper pile. He pulled out two glasses and wiped one on his shirt. He cracked the seal on the bottle and I didn't know what it was. I never seen a sealed bottle before. My father said a sealed bottle ain't no good to nobody. Funny, I still remember some of the things he used to say. Packard poured some in the two glasses, handed one to my father, and kept the one he wiped for himself.

"So, Joe," he said, "how are ya? What've you been doin' all these years?"

"Well, Jake, I been busy, and awhile back I was doing pretty good, but I been on hard times till I started my new job selling shoes. Guy I know started a company and he's a friend of mine and we're in the business together. Business got his name because it was my idea and his money, and you know what that means."

They laughed. Packard looked at me and pointed a big hand at the chair against the wall beside the doorway. When I sat down, the chair scraped the wall a little and they both looked at me.

"So, Joe, who's the kid?"

My father looked at me like he was a little mad. He never did like to start a new story in the middle of another one.

"Well, he's on account of when I was traveling in Oklahoma selling blankets to the Indians."

"What did ya do? Show 'em how to use 'em?"

They both laughed again. My father told the story about my mother again, and I didn't listen. I was looking through the doorway into the next room. I could see a round thing as big as a trash can on a table in there, and I thought I heard something move in it. I couldn't figure it out, and I was thinking about it hard for awhile.

"Hey," said Packard. I looked over and he was talking to me. "Hey," he said again, "Joe says you were born in June. That true? When's your birthday?"

I looked at my father. He looked at me and didn't say anything. "Yesterday was my birthday," I said, "when you were fighting Christenson."

"Is he playing straight with me?" Packard said to my father.

I looked at my father to see if he would say something about it. He just nodded and took another drink.

"Hell, kid," Packard said, and took another glass from a drawer. "Even if your birthday was yesterday, take some of this."

He poured till the glass was half full and held it out to me. I had to get up to get it and then sit down again. Packard held his glass up. My father did too. They waited for me, and I finally held mine up too.

"Fill that with nothing," he said, and took a long pull from his glass. My father did too. I drank, and it tasted kinda smoky at first, but it burned going down, and right under my ribcage it felt like the sun when you sleep on the grass in the summer time. It rose up and stung in my nose, and my eyes watered, so I put it back down.

Packard and my father was laughing.

"Shit, Joe, he drinks like you the first time."

They laughed again and took a little sip. My father looked at Packard.

"Jake, so how you doin'? I wondered what happened to ya."

"Been fighting. I fight pretty regular and I do pretty good."

I heard a fluttering in the other room and wondered about it while I took more sips from the glass. The streets was lit now, and I could see a little better in the other room. The round thing was shaped like a bullet, only about a foot and a half high and a foot wide, with a towel over it, on a low yellow table by a bed. I couldn't see much more.

My father was saying, "For awhile, we were at K.C. I was assistant editor on a newspaper."

I took some more sips from the glass and it was empty, and I set it on the floor real careful. It clinked and fell over and rolled against the wall.

Packard and my father looked at me.

"It's in there, kid." He pointed at a doorway and smiled.

I got up and walked into the next room, and they was laughing behind me. I looked over my shoulder and my elbow banged the door-jamb. My leg brushed the bed. There was a streetlight right outside the bathroom window, and I could see everything real fine. I didn't feel so good, so I put my head down.

When I came out, my nose was dripping and burning inside, and my eyes was wet and it was hard to see. I heard the fluttering again and I was wondering about what was under the towel, so I sat on the edge of the bed to take a look. I started to lift the edge of the towel, when a book slid off the pillow onto the floor. I dropped the towel down and looked in the other room. Neither Packard or my father seen what I was up to. I bent down and picked the book up. It was a book of poems by a guy named Robinson. No kidding. J. J. Packard and my father was still talking, and I slid the book under the pillow. The book bumped something and I lifted the pillow up to see.

It was a gun. It was open, so I could see there was three slugs in it, and three more on the bed. I put the pillow down and looked into the other room. They didn't see me, and I stood up careful and walked around the bed and back into the room where my father and Packard was drinking. I sat in the chair again and leaned over to set the glass up right, and I had to push myself back up with my hand on the floor.

"I'm tired of it, Joe," said Packard. "I'm old and I'm stiff in the morning. I don't sleep too good neither. Sometimes I feel pretty beat to the wide, and I'm tired of it. They used to put me up against some competition but you seen what happened yesterday. That wasn't nothing to be proud of."

"Shit, Jake, you knocked that big dumb Swede out of the ring! Wham!" said my father, crouching over his chair like he couldn't sit still.

"Yeah, he thinks too much. Worries about later while I'm hitting him now."

My father laughed and stood up. He walked through the doorway to the bathroom. Packard finished his glass and wiped it out again. He poured some in my father's glass and then filled up his own again. He looked at me for a minute like he was gonna say something, but my father walked in the room and he just took another drink.

"What's that under the towel, Jake?"

"A bird."

"A bird? You kiddin' me?"

Packard stood up and went in the other room. He came back with a towel in one hand and a bird cage in the other. The bird was a little brown one. It was scrawny and one wing stuck out funny. The cage was all shiny and silver and new.

"Found it almost froze to death by the railroad tracks and I felt kinda sorry for it."

My father looked at the bird and then at Packard kinda funny. Packard seen it.

"What was it?" he said.

"Nothin,' Jake."

"Don't cost anything to feed. Mrs. Bell brings bread crumbs and scraps."

"Yeah," my father said.

Packard stuck his finger between the bars and touched the bird on the head. The bird blinked but it didn't peck his finger.

"Name's Henry. After my father," said Packard.

My father looked at the bird. Packard set the cage on the table and they started talking about Chicago where they grew up and people I never heard of, so I leaned back and closed my eyes. I guess I musta fell asleep.

"C'mon, kid. Let's go," my father said. He was kicking at the chair leg, and my head was bumping the wall. I stood up and rubbed my eyes. My father walked over to the door to the hallway and went out. Packard leaned against the door frame, listening to my father in the hall.

"You sure, Jake?" my father was saying. "A good fighter needs a good trainer. Remember how it was?"

Packard just stood there with a far-off look on his face. I went out in the hall and he slapped me on the shoulder.

"So long, kid. Good drinking with ya," he said. "So long, Joe."

"So long, Jake," said my father, and went walking down the hall. I followed him to where the corner was and looked back. Packard was watching me and held up his hand and nodded. I waved, and he backed into the room and shut the door.

My father led the way down the two flights and back to the front door. A door on the side was open and somebody was singing in there. My father looked and then leaned in the doorway. I couldn't see anything from where I was.

"G'night, Mrs. Bell," he said.

I heard her walk to the doorway. She was still wearing the green dress, but she took the apron off.

"Well, you're up pretty late," she said.

She looked over his shoulder.

"And with the boy, too."

"He's all right," said my father. "On the train to St. Louis, he stayed awake the whole time waitin' to cross the Mississippi. He's crazy for seein' rivers."

"Well, he must be pretty tired out now," said Mrs. Bell. "G'night, mister. What's your name again?"

"Shepard," said my father. "Joe Shepard."

I hadn't heard that one before.

"G'night," Mrs. Bell said to me.

"G'night," I said.

My father opened the door and I went out. He was standing on the top step, and Mrs. Bell was closing the door, when we heard a shot. I heard the tinkle of glass falling in the alley beside the rooming house. We all looked at each other, standing real still.

"What was it?" said Mrs. Bell. She held her breath and raised her head, listening.

Then there was another shot, and I jumped and ran back in and up the stairs. My father bolted in behind me. Mrs. Bell was yelling to the other tenants as she followed us. When I was halfway up the second set of stairs, I heard the last shot. I turned the two corners and ran to the door of Packard's room.

It wasn't locked, and I pushed it open and ran into the room. I looked around and the bird cage was gone. Everything else was the same. I looked in the bedroom. It was dark and the bathroom door was shut. I ran in and opened it.

Packard was sitting on the crapper, leaning on the wall, and his arms was back so I couldn't see his hands. His eyes was open, and they was looking at me, and his skull was gone above the eyebrows. I felt it all coming up again and looked at the floor. The gun was there between his feet, and the bird cage was in there, and feathers and blood were everywhere. The bottle was on the windowsill and the window was busted out. The wood on one side was splintered and cracked. I could smell that dusty smell of old wood split open, and something else, just barely, from the red running down the wall behind Packard. I didn't look at it again.

I heard my father and Mrs. Bell run into the room, but I didn't move until my father pulled me out of the way.

"Jesus, Mary, and . . . ," he whispered.

"Oh, my God," said Mrs. Bell. "I wish—" She looked at me and then my father.

"Oh, my God," she said again, and started to cry, putting her head down in her fists.

My father was staring at Packard.

"Go get a cop, kid," he said. "Go on! Go!"

I ran out of the room and down the hallway, pushing through the people starting to crowd around the doorway. They was all asking me questions, but I just kept pushing through. I still felt sick and my eyes was tearing from keeping it down. I got to the front door and people came streaming in.

"What happened, kid? Where is it?"

I pointed behind me and they ran up the stairs.

I ran out on the stoop and yelled for the cops. Some people in the street turned around and looked at me when they heard me yelling. I yelled louder and some of them started yelling too. Pretty soon a cop came running up the steps. His uniform was real new and stiff.

"What is it, kid? What?"

He had a nightstick in his hand, and when he grabbed me by the shoulders, the shaft knocked me on the side of my head.

"Upstairs," I said. "A man shot himself."

He looked over my shoulder at the stairs.

"Jesus," he said.

He let go of me and ran into the rooming house. I heard his feet pounding up the stairs. Then the door slammed behind him.

I sat down and crossed my arms over my knees and put my chin down. It was pretty warm outside, but I was shaking. I wondered about it all then, and I still want to know why somebody like J. J. Packard would do something like that. He was a real fighter. He never quit till he won. That's what the insiders said. A man who could take on anybody don't seem like a man who would end up dead in a bathroom with the top of his head blown off. A lot of people say he musta been crazy, but he didn't look crazy to me. And he did it anyway. I remember thinking I was glad he didn't do it on my birthday. At least I still had that.

Zach Savich

ANIMAL

I wash everything on as hot as it can be. My old towel

still hangs by the bath, never drying. The steam itself
is a shower curtain, and my sweat presses back as fast as I
    wash—this body's

a *waste*, as in, plain, an *expanse*, yet I feel such a pleasant
    strumming in my personal

surfaces, our ongoing passionate disaster, these meanings that
    rub one foot
against its other three times unavoidably at the instant

directly abutting dozing, of long legs and a low fence, and one
    thing always

staying behind to leave, so therefore we are not the problem.

I know all prayers should end in fire or a river, and everything I
    say begins
with its hortation implied: I like that the word itself means *let us*
and that it appears tied to *hours* and *ahora*, *now*, therefore,
aloha, and: *allors*. The allurements of these features uphold me,
days we have spent fixing fences that, in Jill's phrase,
lean now like old dogs, (I see them, and *now*, as actually leaning *in*
her phrase, voice, situated extant there), as these days
    themselves begun certainly

coming together in exhaustion, once we have worked in sun

and swum in the pond, and imagined at once, aloud, so to
   speak,
as you were saying, you get my drift, you're telling me.

BILL THE LOTTERY GOD

It was in all the papers and on TV. Every house in the Third District built after 1910 and not restored or commercially rezoned after 1960 qualified for a free paint job by the state. Homeowners could also get low-interest home-improvement loans to fix up the interior on their own. New appliances, floors, wallpaper, the works. The only catch was that they had to provide an "artifact."

"Keepsakes of the state's past," the newspapers called them, whether dug up from the yard or kept for years in the attic. These artifacts, once authenticated, would go to the creation of relic rooms in West Virginia's thirty one state-run museums—all part of a campaign to preserve the state's past.

"This legislation gives landmark-like status to each and every of our old homes, whether you're rich or poor," Senator Dove said on TV.

Not everyone, my father among them, was convinced. Dad was quick to call the legislation more social welfare, just another handout to the blacks. But by the weekend, he was as eager as everyone else to see the spectacle taking place next door in the poor little town of Bolivar. Damn jiggaboos were digging up the place, he said, looking for artifacts.

My older brother Robbie wanted to go along, so naturally I did too, and just like that, we all piled in the car. Mom was going as well. She was as concerned as our father. The town of Bolivar was nothing but run-down houses built after 1910. If artifacts of any number were found in that town's soil, historic Harpers Ferry and its national park, also in the Third District, would have serious competition.

Up the long hill we pulled, our '93 Ford Escort Wagon reluctant to make the climb. This was Dad's U.S. mail car, unloaded. Since our county didn't have regular mail vans, carriers like my father had to use their own personal vehicles, as much as the union was trying to change this. In the back window, making it official, was a hand-lettered, cardboard sign—U.S. Mail.

Mom had her knees together and her eyes on the hundreds of grungy rubber bands around the signal column. Fat ones. Thin ones. Red and white ones. So many there was no more signal column to see or grip.

This little collection said nothing of the other weird things Dad had in the car, hanging or stuffed, wedged or arranged somehow—Civil War bullets in the ashtray, loaded .45 under the seat along with a bottle of brandy, and a package of Nutter Butter cookies he told us to stay the hell out of.

Robbie was next to me in the backseat, a leaking burlap sack of mule oats between us. He had on his stupid reindeer hat, its yellow felt antlers sticking up in the back window.

No one said a word as we rode past town hall, the scene of Senator Dove's crime. Mom had the full story on her lap, the county paper rolled up like the Declaration of Independence to keep with us for the last day on earth.

At Tarton Street, just across the Bolivar line, Dad took his foot off the gas. Just beyond the Senator's new sign for *Shenandoah Valley History Preservation League* was the spectacle everyone was talking about. From shabby house to shabby house, poor black kids were digging up their yards, vacant lots, and patches of weedy ground wherever they could find them. Using hoes, broom handles, even the legs off an ironing board, they were popping holes from street to street, unearthing everything not made of dirt, looking for that precious artifact to bring home like a nugget of gold.

Dad couldn't help but laugh. Without a metal detector and little guidance, he said, these dumb kids couldn't find a Mountain Dew bottle cap. And if there were so-called artifacts in Bolivar, he went on to say, then everybody knew they came from the Harpers Ferry's armory and mills.

Mom said he could be crass and laugh all he wanted, but Senator Dove was bringing in a team of state archeologists to help supervise the effort in both towns.

"Good lord," she said, "look at them all."

Across the horizon, it was like harvest time, only there were no beans or potatoes to dig, just bare yards with bike frames stuck in them. Mom had her pocketbook up on her lap as if ready to give a donation.

"I wonder if it's happening on the other streets?" Robbie asked.

"Well, you know it is," Dad was quick to say.

Why, every weedy lot from Hog Alley to Bluefield had a piece of pig iron in it. The whole crazy matter, he said, could be put to rest by taking a well-drilling machine behind the fire hall and dropping a fifty-foot hole in the middle of the carnival grounds, and if there was a big clank, followed by a broken drill bit, then we had found the solid gold head of Frederick Douglass buried there by the Hoover regime. He was completely serious about this, too.

Ahead, shirtless black kids were out on every corner, hacking sticks and baseball bats at what was left of the sidewalk, stopping only to gawk at whitey coming through.

"Bill," Mom said, giving a long, pensive look out the window, "can't something be done?"

"Be done?" he said, looking over at her. "Sounds like a hell of a lot's being done already."

Thanks to her Senator Dove, he said, the NAACP was opening a third and fourth chapter in the Panhandle. They were already behind every public funding decision and now had their fingers in a new wing of the Old Charles Town Library.

My father, you see, didn't like black people or their towns, but he didn't much like our white neighbors in Harpers Ferry either. We had one of the last private residences down the hill, in the so-called historic tract. Jammed around us were a hundred tacky souvenir shops, over-sized park buildings, and fancy old Harpers Ferry homes. Over the years, it had a way of crushing us down, making us unfriendly. If we weren't ashamed of our drab little house, we were hostile toward tourists. When Robbie shot a hole in the wax museum window across the street with a pellet gun and nicked the figure of John Brown across the pants leg, Dad asked how come he didn't aim for the head.

"But what these damn goofs need is a metal detector," he went on to say, pointing across the dash, seeing an entirely different town at its worst. "Look, that damn boy's using his mother's good cane, I bet."

Robbie would have laughed out hard if not for Mom's plastic rosary that, looped over the mirror, was tapping like crazy against the windshield as a kindness reminder.

Jerking on the headrest, I sat up.

"Dad, I can bury that single-shot of yours up here."

My father single-shot me a look in the mirror. Mom turned around in her seat. Robbie kicked out a laugh. Slowly I sat back.

"My good Henry Falling Block Rifle barrel? Oh, no, you don't, mister." I was surprised when, a few seconds later, he looked up in the mirror again and said, "And just *where* you gonna bury it?" Mom was surprised, too. She sat looking at him until we turned onto Jackson Street.

From house to house, blacks were practically swinging their hoes into each other. It was Dawn of the Dead of gardeners. "Minor Miner 49er," the headline in the early edition read. "Artifact Fever!" said county weekly. Mom, awestruck by the sight, commented that it was hard to imagine all these homes in disrepair being painted at the expense of the state. Cost to taxpayers would just have to be astronomical.

"Oh, Katie," our father growled, "Dove's not going to make good on that."

I popped up again. "He's not?"

"Hell, no, it's just an empty political promise to win votes. You watch."

"Not if it's legislated," Robbie chimed in.

Dad gave my smartass brother a frown. That was my cue to lean forward again.

"How about those wooden parts off that one gun? You have a couple extra of those."

He looked up in the mirror. "Wooden parts?"

"He means forearm caps," Robbie said.

Dad's voice rose into a truck tire whine—"My good forearm caps? *No way.* I spent a hell of a lot of time epoxying them."

"Oh, Bill, I'm sure you have another one," Mom said, putting her pocketbook back on the dirty floor.

Dad kicked out a funny laugh.

"'Another one,' she says. Katie, there's not 'another one' from Richmond to Appomattox."

Strike two. We rode on quietly.

My father collected old guns. He had a few good ones, including a 1689 flintlock musket made somewhere in England and a 1921 Lansing fowling piece last owned by Howard Taft's granddaughter, supposedly. But most were broken up, parts really—barrels, stocks, triggers. He tried to put them together from time to time, but he was no gunsmith.

Farther into Bolivar we rode. Along the road with shovels over their shoulders were shiny black men who looked like they had walked out of the Dust Bowl, and in the fields were more kids digging around junked cars. Dad looked up in the mirror at me again.

"Besides, whose damn yard you gonna bury it in? You haven't answered me that?"

While Robbie and I traded glances, Mom looked over at Dad.

"Bill?"

"Well, Katie, I'm just supposing—and besides, this just goes to show you how damn knuckleheaded the idea is. I mean, who benefits? You can't just pick and choose."

"Well, apparently everyone benefits," said my mother, looking down at the paper.

"Not everyone is gonna find a damn artifact," Dad said back.

Mom went on staring a hole into the side of his head.

"And what the hell constitutes an artifact anyway?" he asked, squirming out of the moment.

I reached around the seat, snatched the paper off my mother's lap, and scanned it.

"An artifact is defined," I read, "as a man-made or shaped object at least one hundred years old."

"*Shaped* object?" Dad said.

He looked over at Mom for help.

"Like an agate, I imagine," she said.

"Broken or intact," I added.

Dad spun halfway around in the seat. "That's what it says?"

Robbie, his antlers bobbing over my shoulder, confirmed it, and Dad repeated the words, broken or intact, over and over, as we turned onto Simón Bolívar Avenue. At that moment, we all had the same thought—our house was the Home Depot of broken artifacts.

I tried again.

"What about all your old barrels then?"

This time my father had a question for me.

"Damn it, Josh, why are you so all-fired eager?"

Robbie let out a laugh, and I sat back.

Why *was* I so eager? I looked down at the county paper, at the words across the newsprint that told of all the unhappy Harpers Ferry residents—of all the outrage and threats of laws suits. Why? Simple. *Revenge.* My poor family had been stared at, pointed at, gawked at, smirked at, and scowled at by the snooty people of Harpers Ferry for too long.

But there was another reason, a reason I had to keep secret, and her picture was in my wallet. *Shanice.*

On Simón Bolívar Avenue, we came to a section of shanties and closed-up shops that were a sight to pity, including a Dairy Queen and Stanley Hardware flaking away in the sun. Mom had no kind words for the county commissioner for putting Washington Concrete, the main employer in this area, out of business. Even Dad agreed that they could have at least turned the old block buildings into an A&P or Wal-Mart, to give the area a little local economy.

Robbie scooted down in the seat, bringing his knees up against the back of the front seat. I let my head fall against the window. All the while, the rosary went on tapping, still working the Christian angle.

We headed out into the hills, crossing railroad tracks my mother remembered as being smoother at one time. Past dried-up orchards the road rose and dipped, sending my mother into a brief, sad history of the apple industry that the illustrious LeMaster's had abandoned in Bolivar. This, I realized, was my mother working on herself angle.

Then Dad made a few turns he thought would put an end to the Bolivar issue by leading us to the new highway, but he instead drove us straight toward a high chain-link fence.

"What the hell?" he said, brakes squeaking.

Robbie sat up and peered ahead, antlers like dual periscopes.

"Tennis court, golf course, lake—*Nakakoji Land Development*," he read off a sign.

Mom leaned forward to get a better view.

"Lakefront Home Sites available," she read. "Equestrian facilities by appointment or reservation only."

From this spot in the road, the difference between the haves and have nots in the world couldn't have been clearer. Inside the fence: spotless grass, trees that looked cloned, no broken glass. Outside: patchy, yellowed grass, litter galore, cracked-up roadway.

Just then, a small white pickup with yellow lights on top pulled up beside us from behind. *Sunrise Hills Security*, it said on the door. The fat-faced guard gawked over at us in our sagged-down little car.

"Bill, he wants you to leave."

"I know he does," Dad grumbled. "The hell with him."

We pulled on slowly, down the service road toward the security kiosk, looking for a spot to turn around, all the while with this self-important little truck right on our bumper. Our muffler scraped, and the car cut off twice in one of the worst three-point turns in history, but finally we got headed back the way we came in, escorted away as one of the local unworthies.

No one said a word as we were chased back into familiar Bolivar scenery, tail between our legs. We turned left, past a burnt-out laundry van, then right, down a dirt street full of little aluminum-siding houses every shade of blue and gray. Fat old women on porch swings, seeing poor white folks coming through, stood and gawked over the railing. From under car hoods, shiny black men peered.

Then, something extraordinary happened. When one waved, another did. Then another. And before we knew it, half the street was waving at my father. He gave one a reluctant wave, then another, and soon he was smiling, even forced to laugh, saying he didn't know a damn one of them, but maybe they knew him somehow. Robbie had the answer. It was the U.S. Mail sign in our back window. Black people always waved to the mailman, he said.

I knew an opportunity when I saw it. I leaned forward.

"How about those rusted up bayonets, Dad?"

Dad shot his eyes up in the mirror.

"Or just one of them?" I said.

Robbie came up beside me.

"Dad, they're probably worthless anyway, being so degraded."

"Bill, your son's right," said Mom, pitching in hard. "You know those things are just extra trouble in our house."

Dad hit the gas to silence us all, but since we were the last old car on the road with valve rattle, there was no silence about it. Ahead stood Bolivar's decrepit municipal building. Behind it, and impossible to miss, was a twenty-foot heap of everything under the sun: parts of bicycles, pieces of picket fences, even a car chassis. This phenomenon was in the morning paper, too. Bolivar residents were asked to stack their artifacts for authentication behind the town hall.

Dad, his curiosity over junk too much, pulled over for a look-see. As he did, he hit a pothole so mammoth that the lead bullets in his ashtray popped high and free like popcorn. That sent him cussing and groping to catch them before bringing the car to hard, squeaky stop, bottle of brandy under the seat clinking. After picking up bullets off the floor, he was out of the car, Robbie and me following.

Behind the Bolivar town hall building, we stood before the huge pile of junk. From tomato stakes to bottle tops, every scrap of lumber and tin from three decades of small-town decay was represented. Names of their recent discovers were either chalked on, painted on, or scratched on, using every sort of identifying mark from initials and birthdates to phone numbers. Someone had even used a soldering iron to put a license plate number on the side of an old mailbox.

As we stood there gawking, on the far side of the pile, black kids were dragging up what anybody could see was nothing but rusted raingutter, though in better condition than what was falling off our house.

Mom spoke first.

"Oh, Bill, this is utterly pathetic. Can't you do something?"

In the pile were some of the town's good water pipes, no doubt pulled up by goofy kids thinking they had found an extra long Civil War gun barrel or something. There was even a sewer pipe mistaken for a cannon barrel.

"Look," I said, using my toe to move a piece of board. "Our St. Joseph's thermometer."

Or one just like it. Still attached to its tinny yellow stand, it lay in the clutter, the little figure of Jesus smiling up with open arms, a staff of mercury in his hand.

But our mother found something worse than that.

"What in the world?" she said, pointing down.

Robbie bent down to inspect it. Using a clothes hanger lying nearby, he rolled the little head-shaped object into the sunlight. Stamped on its noggin, beside a slot for coins, was *John Brown the Abolitionist!* I knew what it was—a piggy bank. All the banks in the area gave them out. This one had been spray-painted black, to make it look like an artifact. There were two more of them, half crushed in the pile.

Slowly we got back into the car and pulled off, not saying a word. Coasting up to a stop sign, Dad sat staring out the window, looking lost in a spell. Mom's eyes met his somewhere in the distance, it seemed. Finally he looked up in the mirror at Robbie and me.

"You damn boys still haven't answered my question. Whose yard?"

"All of them?" I said, shrugging.

"Katie," he said, looking over at her, "suppose they get caught?"

"We won't," promised Robbie.

"Suppose they do one of those, whatta you call it, 'forensic digs' and find out you all planted my good guns?"

"Oh, Bill, I doubt they'll go to all that trouble."

He let out his funny laugh. "'Go to all that trouble,' she says."

"Then you'll get the credit," I said, bright-voiced.

Dad shot me a look. He didn't appreciate my attitude, or my point.

We pulled on. The car returned to groaning, and Dad to shaking his head.

"All right," he said at last.

My brother and I popped up in the seat.

"Robbie, Josh, that trigger guard off the busted-up Winchester. If you two wanna bury something, bury that." He looked over at Mom before she could look back at him. "That should qualify as a damn artifact."

"Whose yard?" I asked, yanking on his headrest.

"Yes, whose yard, Bill?" Mom said, with a grim bearing in her voice I didn't understand. "I really wanna know how you'll decide this."

She sat staring a hole into the side of his head again. If he was playing Bill the Lottery God, then she was curious how he would decide whose ship would come in. He actually had an answer.

"Whoever in the hell can displease Lee Jackson or Mike Smallwood the most by getting a new roof and driveway—that's who," he said.

Mom's voice spiraled out like a paper airplane. "Ooh, wow, Bill, you hear what you're encouraging?"

He did, and he could live with it just fine. I could too, and was quick to make suggestions, complete with alternates. Terrell Washington, I said. He had to work in Lee Jackson's hot restaurant kitchen all day. His family was definitely deserving. This was my third choice, by the way, not my first. I was working my way backward, warming my father up. Or wearing him down, depending on how you looked at it.

"Not enough," Dad said after a moment, shaking his head.

"Not enough?" said Mom, kinked up in disbelief. "Bill?"

The car picked up speed. Both McDonald boys, I said, were falsely arrested by Chief Remington recently. That was suggestion two.

Dad thought about this. "Maybe."

"Maybe?" Mom was shaking her head. "Bill, this is not funny."

I sat up even more.

"Charlene Sharpe has the same cancer Grandma had."

Mom spun to me, Dad turned to her, Robbie kicked me in the leg, and the car fell silent. We rode on. I had pushed too far, crumbled the sandcastle with one too many pats.

A quarter of a mile later, we were crossing back into Harpers Ferry, passing the oldest, finest houses. All had big names. "Our Lady of Longstreet" was a yellow mansion with curvy white columns. "McClellan's Charge" and "Burnside's Brigade" were also imposing structures. Dad hated all their owners. Back when he was still delivering mail by foot, if they weren't complaining about all the junk mail he stuffed into their solid-brass antique mailboxes, inscribed with hoity-toity family names, then he was catching the shirttails of his uniform on their fancy fleur-de-lie-pointed gates, all while Fifi the Poodle was yakking at him for doing his job which he got no thanks for.

You never saw so much wealth in your life, he'd often said. Imported dogwood trees, leaded-glass rose windows, security lights and alarm systems. Then, these muckety-mucks had the gall to complain when he brought them an overdue postage slip for ten or twelve cents.

Suddenly, Mom pointed to the far side of the road, where Bolivar people weren't the only ones digging up their town. Mr. Sullivan, a past mayor of Harpers Ferry, was poking a turf edger around his yard, and Mr. Lancaster was letting his brand-new, self-propelled Frogzilla Rottotiller grind in place. Shovels, digging irons, post-hole diggers—all were set out in yards in readiness.

"Well, these damn people aren't entitled," Dad was quick to gripe, nodding around at all the nice Harpers Ferry houses obviously restored after 1960. "What in the hell do they think they're doing?"

Mom was staunchly behind him. No, they certainly didn't qualify. The nerve. As Dad sat looking around, disgusted all the more by the all stinking wealth, Robbie's timing couldn't have been better. My doofus brother sat up and started reading from the paper.

"Bolivar ranks as one of state's poorest eight towns, with a median family income in 2002 of $16,041, below the national poverty line of $18,100 for a family of four. Harpers Ferry, by contrast, ranks as one of the state's top-five richest towns, with a whopping $70,313 median family income. It is roughly 90 percent white, compared to Bolivar's 60 percent African American and 30 percent Hispanic. Nearly half of Harpers Ferry's 750 residents are nonnative, compared to Bolivar's 5 percent."

Dad was looking up in the mirror at my brother as if he had just read from a gay-friendly version of the King James Bible.

"Katie, you hear this. Nearly *two-thirds* of Harpers Ferry's residents are *nonnative?*"

There was a second of silence as Mom looked back at him.

"Yes, Bill, and I think it's even more than that by now."

He craned his neck at her.

"*More?*"

"Well, Bill, you know we're one of the last families this far down the hill."

With an air of indifference, she sat back in the seat and resumed looking straight ahead. Dad glanced at her a few more times before looking up at me.

"Charlene Sharpe," he said. "Katie, isn't that the woman who works as a cook up at the junior high?"

I sat riveted on my mother, waiting for her reply.

"Used to, Bill. I don't believe she works now."

Dad shot her a look.

"Doesn't work?"

"No, she was laid off. I'm sure of that."

Our father was clearly bothered by this. He looked up in the mirror at me again.

"And she has the same cancer as your grandmother?"

I nodded.

"How do you know?"

Robbie gave me a big shove.

"Cause he's in love with her daughter!" he blurted out, grinning.

Dad, his face rigid, didn't like hearing this, not one little bit, whether it was true or not, which it couldn't be. Mom, meanwhile, was looking out the window, her face now struck with a new concern.

"And she can't have any insurance, not working," she said.

"So how in the hell can she ever pay for cancer treatments?"

Mom sat staring off. More beautiful houses, one after another. They just kept coming.

"I don't know."

"So," Dad said, "she *could* use our help then?"

She looked over at him. He looked over at her. You could level your best pictures with the line between their eyes. All that was right and wrong in the world hung in the balance.

But it would take a column of fancy Harpers Ferry cars coming through to help shove Dad over the charity fence for good. When Dr. Smallwood's Volvo came flying past and cut back in without signaling, our father flew into a torrent of cuss words.

"All right," he said, looking up in the mirror at me just before he pulled over to turn the car around, "show me where this Ms. Charlene Sharpe lives."

David Dodd Lee

Calendar Series I: Wolf Spider

It was raining inside
that picture on the wall

and the single tree
had a brown side backing a red
lacquer of trembling

leaves

an exodus

a consciousness quick on its legs

so it was with these stabs
of things seen through the wakefulness in this other boy

his vertebrae tingling

the frame emitting pure static

(inside it a freight
train shook all the milkweeds)

the briars so bad even her socks were bloody

stuck in the neck on a thorn in that single tree

I did check the bedroom

now the windows were open

the fist with no thumbnail had swelled even larger

David Dodd Lee

CALENDAR SERIES I: ROMANTIC

you
and the weather inside you

the Graham crackers the blue jay flips and eats

lack of love

after all that's your head in the window

looking out

through rain
through snow

lonely lonely

one of the new jobs we have is dating

you work in reality TV

the myth of the soul mate

the new staircase covered with sub-prime money

then carpet (chiropractor green)

is part of it ...

couples holding hands with silk over their nude bodies
    streaming
past stars during Ascension ...

erase it all remember the scotch pine and the shovel in the snow

driving with Kim

the way the flakes dimpled
the surface of our cups of hot chocolate

they shredded the moon again she said about the falling snow

David Dodd Lee

Calendar Series I: Porcelain

The doors keep
accumulating

address: wouldn't you like to know

we're lost in our own country

a mouth full of trees gagging on blue water

barrette or a cigarette

it's Friday, a repast,
a sympathy like glass

and that's how you are sumptuous

(hardening with acumen—
after a while the roof just caves in)

what's hidden
what's only

the spinnerets

your damaged handcuffs

go ahead, let him touch you

bees wake in an attic
and aren't worried
about self-esteem

I love that you are in biting range

David Dodd Lee

Calendar Series I: The Pyramids

you were born with a moral sense

which is why the dry colored leaves
swirling in autumn
bring tears

one by one they burdened the enormous blocks
closer and closer to heaven

a wick of blood for your name

you can see it in the bubbles in this rum and Coke

I only felt a peculiar sense it was something
like an island, the Cape

the softest murdering
reason has invented

the way the arm breaks off

buried in the ocean floor

palatial mansion for the bluest barbed wire

the sound of money
reproducing itself
in a vault under the floor in the northwestern-most

bathroom

They have a floor but no eyes

you boil them alive

who wouldn't have a nervous breakdown

Charles R. Gillespie

A Rest for the Weary

Between the final day of high school and the first day of college, every young man who goes from one to the other is faced with a series of weeks, amounting in the end to approximately three months, during which he must prepare himself for this most important exploration into serious scholarship. For some, the effort is comparatively simple and routine. Their fathers or grandfathers will have already assembled some form of wealth and they have only to remain alive and otherwise conscious to assure themselves of a lifetime of pleasure, big-game trophies, licked boots and genuine self-respect for a job well done.

For others, Jack Desbrough included, the task can be made considerably more difficult by the tyrannies—some tiny and some imposed—associated with employment. There are only three positions worth having, and those three are permanently filled. A few others offer some opportunity for advancement and financial reward, providing the young man is willing to mortgage the best years of his life and keep his nose clean.

It took very little time or effort for Bicycle Bob, even in his feebling state, to tell Jack these things and to convince Jack he was destined for a better life than that of wage slave or employee. Jack did not believe his apprenticeship at the bicycle shop had prepared him for many of the usual occupations, but the wise lad had to agree he was too good for them even if it had.

Consequently, Jack was quite prepared to sit out the summer listening to Bicycle Bob during the afternoons and to his weary comrades trudging homeward from their work on pipelines, drilling rigs, and other hot metals during the evenings. For several hours each day, until the sun began seeping through the tin roof in the horizon over his head, Jack would consider his future. Whenever he drifted near discouragement—he never actually became discouraged—Jack would talk with Bicycle Bob. If his mentor's words were not encouragement enough, Jack had only to look at his tiring and aging friends to know he had made the correct decision. Even Max Murphy, who ordinarily enlisted immediately in all of Jack's plans and projects, fell into the employment dodge. Max unloaded bags of cement, heaving them onto his shoulders and carrying them from boxcars into trucks and from trucks into warehouses. Because of his muscles, Max performed every chore—even the purchase of postage stamps—stripped to the waist, so that on each working day he was soon covered from head to foot in gray cement dust. When Max plodded from the T & P tracks down South Lee Street to join Jack and Bicycle Bob he resembled a marvelous, heroic statue freed from the mold and searching for a town square. The gray dust would drift in gentle puffs from his great body and a crowd of small children and happy dogs would trot along behind, waving sticks and United States flags and shouting to envious contemporaries who were not permitted to venture outside their front yards.

At first, Jack and Bicycle Bob reviewed this daily parade without comment although each, in his own way, was quite impressed. Admittedly not so impressed, neither ever felt the urge to unload cement. Gradually, however, the two of them grew uneasy around Max's prosperity. From the casual friend and nephew they had known, he became the owner of a delicately-jeweled wristwatch with a gold-mesh band; from the enthusiastic accomplice, he was transformed into the possessor of a dainty bank book exactly like one treasured by a retired vocal coach.

Jack and Bicycle Bob tried to snatch him back but, true to his character, Max clung stubbornly to what he had begun. It was easy to see that in the same way he had built his muscles and hacked out the convertible, he would now attack employment. One day he might put down the bank book but, if he did, it would only be to begin on another.

"Guess you'll be buying a tennis racquet next," Jack blurted angrily one afternoon. Max blushed and denied the charge, but his protest was weak and unconvincing; and his toes wiggled as though they were already enclosed in canvas shoes.

With regret at the good times past, Jack suggested to Bicycle Bob that the day had come to cease waiting for Max every afternoon. Bicycle Bob readily agreed. The oddly allied pair turned instead to the domino parlors along Grant Avenue. They spent the entire day in those dark temples, so cool the atmosphere clamped on their bones like a mother's chill. Here, Bicycle Bob had taught Jack some of the lessons absorbed so long ago they seemed new again. Here, nothing was changed except change and Bicycle Bob was so skillful at the domino games there was rarely any change in that.

Had anyone measured the distance, they would have discovered the grandest of the shabby parlors was located exactly midway between United States Highway 80 and the Texas and Pacific railroad tracks. Wanderers, including strange troubadours with instruments they could not play and songs they could not sing, would pass through on their route to the California gold fields, bartering and trading with the adventurers who had journeyed no further than their sturdy chairs around the felt-covered table. Sweat was instantly dried here, and good luck exchanged for cash. There was reason enough to leave the place, but not reason enough to go anywhere else.

Once, the unsuspecting Jack was talked into employment while he sat at the elbow of Bicycle Bob and sipped from the old man's can of Pearl. The talker was a flatterer, a knave who dripped names and hints of currency idly through his conversation, using them as casual punctuation: glittering items that floated back-and-forth and slowly hypnotized the dozing Jack.

The fast talker was a former crony of Bicycle Bob and a dandy little man with a pint bottle of Old Crow permanently in the hip pocket of his khaki trousers. He claimed to have played guitar in the finest clubs in New Orleans, to have sailed upon several of the seas, and to have shoveled manure at both the rodeo in Madison Square Garden and at the Fort Worth Fat Stock Show. By profession he was now an iterant street decorator, a rare artist whose work had appeared on principal avenues at important times.

Between the two of them, Jack and the dandy little man spread a rainbow of color over some of the dullest—previously dullest—minor towns and communities in West Texas. They helped celebrate Rattlesnake Derbies, Fourths of Julys, and Old Settlers' Reunions. With a few nails and red, white, and blue bunting they cured eyesores and restored faith in national holidays. The job was a satisfying one and Jack might well have remained forever at his curious position atop ladders and among the oft-maligned tubes of neon few men ever really know or understand. Might have remained there, that is, except for waking up one morning to find the dandy little man gone from the room they had shared in a sunburned, peeling tourist court on the outskirts of Seagraves. The room was incredibly quiet and hot, empty except for Jack and the flies circling noisily around opened cans of pork and beans and sliced pineapple on the dresser top. Jack dressed, slowly, and then walked into the depressing sunshine.

There were no clouds and no indication there would ever be any clouds again. The dandy little man's old brown automobile and the orange trailer full of plead red, white and blue decorations were gone. Jack realized immediately, even though he had not had the experience before, that he had been abandoned, stranded among strangers, without so much as a single paycheck to show for his weeks of employment. He re-laced and re-tied his shoes, then sat upon the porch and leaned back against the screen door of his room. He resisted the impulse to feel sorry for himself and listened instead to the humming of the flies inside and to the traffic, bound north and south, on the highway in front of the tourist court. Jack imagined he could hear the sounds of kitchen doors slamming and firearms being loaded. He stood and walked slowly to the highway, which was also the town's principal thoroughfare. Looking northward, Jack could see the result of his yesterday's work, hanging limply in the breezeless air. Looking southward, he could see the route home. Jack crossed the highway and stood on the edge of the pavement, blotches of the asphalt already softening in the patched areas. He was too proud to use his thumb to signal for a ride, but stood nonchalantly, hands in his Levi pockets. A young United States Marine, a private first class, picked him up, almost immediately.

For several miles, the Marine explained to Jack how he had never taken any crap from any man during his entire life and was not planning to begin now. Jack said he had never taken any crap from anyone either although occasionally it had been given to him. The young Marine said he did not like smart aleck remarks and sometimes considered them crap. Jack wanted the ride home as desperately as he had ever wanted anything and for that reason refrained from elaborating on the argument. Instead, he closed his eyes and lapsed into a reverie of revenge, dreaming of dynamite and similar explosions, followed by parades along boulevards he had decorated himself.

The United States Marine carried Jack to within a half block of Bicycle Bob's favorite domino parlor. Jack found the old man there, almost alone. Entirely along at his table. Bicycle Bob said he was surprised Jack did not already know most of the trouble in the world was caused by feisty rascals like the dandy little man. Jack said he was surprised Bicycle Bob's advice always came after it was needed.

A Mexican sitting at the next table laughed at the spectacle of the storied old advisor and the young apprentice arguing among themselves. Jack and Bicycle Bob frowned at the Mexican, injuring his feelings considerably; or at least the Mexican always insisted his feelings were damaged during later recollections of the afternoon.

The Mexican leaped to his feet, angrily, and shouted, "You think I'm a Mexican don't you?" Jack, rarely startled by anything, including shouting, could not readily respond to the question. As a matter of fact, he did think the Mexican was a Mexican, but it was obviously not the proper response. "I'm Indian," the Mexican said, slamming his Mexican-looking fist down across his chest. "I'm a full-blooded Indian as good as any man in this place."

The Mexican said he had an automobile in excellent running condition and offered to drive Bicycle Bob and Jack out into the country where he would whip the shit out of them, providing they would pay for half of the gasoline. Bicycle Bob said he had no particular craving for having his shit whipped out of him and was not buying any gasoline for crazy greasers even he developed a craving. Jack did not think this was the thing to say, not from fear of having to fight the Mexican so much as a loathing for standing out in the dusty prairie and fighting under a sun undiluted by clouds for thousands of miles. He could imagine lying in the dirt, on his back, while grasshoppers and other jumping and crawling intruders slithered and leaped around his remains.

The Mexican did not seem to resent Bicycle Bob's calling him a greaser, presumably to reinforce his case for Indianhood. Instead, he sat down between Bicycle Bob and Jack and tipped his chair back on its rear legs so he could lean against the graying wall. "Old man," the Mexican said, "We need old men like you in politics. This is the only city in Texas without any corruption in high places. You could fix that."

Jack believed the Mexican to be joking, but Bicycle Bob appeared to take his words seriously and soberly. Before long, the Mexican had obviously become serious. After two hours of intense conversations, Bicycle Bob announced he would be a candidate for Justice of the Peace of Precinct Four. Jack and the Mexican, who said his name was also Bob, would be his campaign committee. The Palace Dominoes was not in Precinct Four, but neither was any other decent accommodation so they named the table they sat around as their campaign headquarters and Bicycle Bob ordered three cans of Pearl, their campaign beer.

Elaborate plans were discussed and developed immediately. Bicycle Bob said he would conduct a bitter campaign. Bob, the Mexican, agreed this was necessary, but added there was no great hurry since no other candidate was likely to challenge for the job. Justices of the Peace were paid a percentage of the fees they collected and Precinct Four was notorious for slender pickings. The last Justice of the Peace had resigned in mid-office, complaining—in the public print—that he was plagued by chiselers who wanted a cut-rate on their wedding ceremonies, bullies who called and threatened to beat him up for sentencing their little brothers to 10 days in jail for malicious mischief, and angry niggers seeking injunctions to keep the Mexicans out of their neighborhoods.

Bob, the Mexican, wanted to begin the campaign with a series of letters to the editor demanding paved streets, lighted thoroughfares, and more Bermuda grass for the South Side, also known as Precinct Four. Bicycle Bob, the candidate, was reluctant. "Nobody reads letters and nobody reads newspapers and double nobody reads letters in newspapers," he said. "What we're going to do is go out and meet the voters, show them some interest. After we've started collecting fees we can worry about good deeds. I'm running for the J.P.'s office. Not for scoutmaster."

Jack, hoping Bicycle Bob was kidding about seriously campaigning, soon lost interest in the conversation. The time for enrolling in college was not far away and, with the taste of dread appearing in his beer, Jack realized his future was no better planned than his past. He had the sensation of being some sort of eccentric fruit which was all peeling. As the fruit was pared away and pared away nothing was ever uncovered, no juicy morsel, not even a seed. He felt sick and walked into the alley to piss on the mound of discarded playing cards, his stream eroding hell out of a deuce of hearts. "I know this isn't the best thing I can do," Jack said aloud. He ignored the two whores, leaning out the hotel window across the alley, shouting "Sweetheart" at him; but he felt better. He felt like a Sweetheart.

A week later, Bicycle Bob walked into the Palace Dominoes carrying two boxes under one arm. Inside the boxes were printed cards in pastel greens, blues, and pinks announcing Bicycle Bob's candidacy for Justice of the Peace of Precinct Four, pleading honesty and integrity, and asking for votes and influence. Bob, the Mexican, wanted to give away something more substantial, an emery board or needled and Bicycle Bob said he might do that during his first re-election campaign, depending upon the fees he collected.

Max Murphy helped distribute some of the cards for his uncle, but the bulk of the labor was assumed by Jack and Bob, the Mexican. They divided Precinct Four between them and set out to place Bicycle Bob's cards in every screen door on the South Side. There were no problems in this sort of campaigning beyond a few dogs who seemed to have been trained at some odd establishment specializing in the protection of the seedy and decrepit. Jack, by nature, was kindly toward animals, but did not hesitate to kick the hell out of any of the dogs who attempted to impede the placing of a card on the master's screen door.

Following each day's work, the campaigners returned to the Palace Dominoes to report to Bicycle Bob. Truthfully, all the reporting was done by Bob, the Mexican, since Jack never had anything of significance to contribute. According to Bob, the Mexican, his appointed routes were filled with housewives who appeared nude at their doorways to accept the cards. The naked women were mostly doctor's wives who usually invited him into their homes where they engaged Bob, the Mexican, in incredible sexual endeavors, some of which took him an hour or two to reconstruct even though touching only on the highlights. Jack could never understand what it was about Bob, the Mexican, to attract so many doctor's wives. He was ugly and meanfaced, as charming as a collection agent. Jack did know his own route was dull and desultory. Instead of naked housewives he encountered illtempered watchdogs and small children featuring filth flowing out of their noses and diapers and down their chins and skinny legs. Only once did he meet a housewife at a backdoor. She threw a basin of soapy water at him, thinking he was some sort of Halloween prankster out on a holiday.

The day he met the housewife who threw dishwater on him, Jack determined to quit politics; but when he arrived at the Palace Dominoes he found Bicycle Bob and Bob, the Mexican, looking so cheerful he told them instead that he had met a housewife who dragged him into the shower with her. The news seemed to please Bicycle Bob and Bob, the Mexican, immensely. Jack suddenly realized he had been meeting doctor's wives all along.

Shortly afterward, Jack and Max, Bicycle Bob and Bob, the Mexican, sat around the table, playing moon and listening to the election returns. There were infrequent reports on Precinct Four Justice of the Peace contest, but those which came through made it obvious Bicycle Bob was going to fail. A schoolhouse janitor named A.C. Jackson, called Ace by the children in the first through sixth grades at South Elementary, was compiling an enormous advantage entirely on write-in votes he had not even solicited. The small group around the table grew quieter as the size of the defeat grew greater. Jack realized he could not care less about Bicycle Bob's embarrassment, but he saw no reason for Bob, the Mexican, to explain that Ace Jackson was winning because the voters did not really know him.

All that remained of the campaign were a number of Bicycle Bob's little cards. The old man took them out of the box and shuffled them, mixing the pastel blues, greens and pinks in an extraordinary pattern on the table. Tears sparkled in the old eyes and Jack, looking away into the people passing on the sidewalk outside, considered the heartbreak of the election count, the certification that you are unnecessary. He was glad the summer was over and hoped Bicycle Bob would not actually cry. Jack knew he would not cry himself, knew he would not waste another summer of his life by working.

Luisa A. Igloria

JOURNEY TO THE WEST

Opening his brown coat, Monkey shook a hundred jewels to the ground.

They shone, pomegranate seeds in moonlight. They pulled
me under their bright sleeves. Of course I wanted to taste.

The wheel turned in the direction of the sun. Faster than a tail flick
the waters rose. Birds scattered ideographs for change. None of this,

ever meant in malice. Marigold heads bent against a scrim of glass.
The instrument approached its vibrato. The payment for a kiss,

in the tumult—not after, but before.
What did it mean, the dense brocade of grass,

the open gate; the tiller that the hand turned
in another direction? I didn't see the goddess pulling the line

across continents in darkness, did not see her face,
lovely and indifferent; my cares, a small boat that drifted on water.

Luisa A. Igloria

The Minim

In a music studio waiting room, waiting
for my daughter to emerge from piano lessons,

I read a magazine article on tubercular
Modigliani—how after his death, his lover Jeanne

leaped to her own from a Paris rooftop, pregnant
with his second child. It was a time

that critics describe as the emergence of
Modernity, the coming-of-age of that inconsolable

and perturbing child who gazes
through window gratings of an apartment

and sees the world fracturing into little cubes of blue.
What a world to have lived in, to have arrived in,

especially for the wayfarer, the exile
with his *portmanteau* of souvenirs, describing

the pavement between the world of no return and the world
of always beginning, and the light that shimmers

somewhere in the dusty trees. A public outcry shut down
his first exhibit, *because it threatened prevailing notions of decency—*

those women's necks lengthening in twilight, their tulip thighs
promising welcome. Not sixty years before,

the painters from Manila made their way to Rome and Barcelona.
Only fifth or sixth class, said Retana of Juan Luna; *no notable place*

among the ranks of Spanish painters. Reviewers said the same
of José Garcia Villa when he came to America to write

among the early Moderns: *at best, a minor poet.*
Modernity, Modernity, how cruel you've been

as Muse, demanding constant servitude and reinvention.
In Luna's *Spoliarium*, the two gladiators dragged from

the arena to the chamber of bodies where they will be
stripped and burned, leave rust-colored tracks upon the floor.

The music teacher, a Russian émigré
who used to be a biophysicist in her former life,

might recognize the paradox: distance
infinitely halved, never sutured close.

"Spoliarium" is a mural by Filipino painter Juan Luna (1857-1899). He was among the cohort of Filipino artists and scholars who went to Europe in the 1800s, where they pondered the problems arising from a corrupt colonial dispensation in the islands, the issues of cultural and linguistic identity, social reform, and a burgeoning Filipino nationalism. Luna entered "Spoliarium" in the Exposicion Nacional de Bellas Artes in 1884, where it won one of two gold medals. In 1886 it was sold for 20,000 pesetas. It currently hangs in the National Museum of the Philippines.

BREATH OF THE WOK

The beginning of the Chinese New Year, the year of the monkey. And it was off to a cold start, a typical winter day in Michigan's Upper Peninsula: sun-starved, winds from the north, the snow on Sunday Lake blue-gray in the dusk. Too *leung*, but Xiaolu had prepared a three-course dinner with dessert, *neen gow*, for his wife and stepson Ricky and in-laws at their bowling alley. A warm traditional celebration meant to restore balance. Sending the old year out, ushering in the new, honoring family and ancestors, tightening the bonds between them.

He regretted not pulling on his coat when he came out to help his father-in-law from the car into the wheelchair. The cold, taxing on the heart muscles. Xiaolu wasn't a stranger to winter weather; he'd lived in Chicago all his life, but it had never seemed this frigid. He was having trouble adjusting, he hadn't expected they would still be here, in this one-stoplight town, running his in-laws' bowling alley. His wife Kari had come north after her father's heart attack last spring, leaving Xiaolu and Ricky to finish out the school year. A temporary rearrangement of their lives. The plan had been for them to return home in the fall—back to school, to work, to normal. And a new beginning: trying to get pregnant, expanding the family circle. This had been the original plan. He dreamed of being a "Baba," a real father, not a step away. But now when he tried to picture his family's future, everything seemed scattered, like pins knocked down by a ball.

Inside the bowling alley was almost balmy, the old furnace working double-time and clanging every now and then. The air smelled spicy, full of lemon zest and ginger and soy sauce and scallions and baking fish. A couple of bowling balls hummed down the lanes. Only Ricky and his friend Matt were playing. Richard struggled out of the wheelchair, and Xiaolu tried to help, but his father-in-law waved him off. Xiaolu showed his in-laws to the table he'd set by the bar, and Richard walked over, using a hand-carved diamond willow cane. He could negotiate inside without much difficulty, but Ethel walked alongside with one finger hooked through a belt loop.

Kari took their coats, caps, gloves, and scarves, and went to hang them up in the back, and Xiaolu opened a bottle of plum wine and one of sparkling grape juice. He called Ricky and Matt over, poured their drinks, and began pouring the wine. Ethel told him Richard couldn't have any, but Richard said, "Ah, nonsense. Pour away, Lou. It's a special occasion." They called him Lou, everyone in Wakefield called him that.

Ethel gave him a tight smile and held up two fingers, pressed together. He nodded and poured small shots in their glasses.

Kari came back. "Why don't we get started," she said and motioned to Xiaolu. "I'll grab the soup while you get the salmon."

"In a moment." Xiaolu moved over to her, handed her a wine glass. He lifted his and said, "*Gung Hay Fat Choy*. It's a traditional New Year's greeting." He wasn't certain he was pronouncing it correctly; it had been years since he'd used it. Auntie Ming had taught him.

Ricky and Matt tried saying, "*Gung Hay Fat Choy*," but said it sounded funny.

"Try this, boys," Richard said. "*Onnellista Uutta Vuotta toivottaa.*" They groaned, but Xiaolu attempted the Finnish version. "Not half-bad," his father-in-law said and held up his empty glass. Xiaolu gave him another splash of wine and they toasted, the glasses pinging against each other.

"It seems different in here," Ethel said, her voice raspy from too many years of smoking. "Bigger somehow," she said. "Or maybe smaller." It was the first time she'd been there since Richard's relapse in late August.

"What do you think?" Kari asked her parents. "Xiaolu's been busy all day getting everything ready. Doesn't it look great?" She put her hand on his forearm and gave it a squeeze.

He'd put out a few bowls of oranges and tangerines, along with a platter of candy and snacks, traditional foods for ringing in the New

Year with a few non-traditional substitutions, and the boys had drawn pictures of monkeys on red construction paper.

"I like the decorations," Ethel said. "Bold and fiery. What does it all mean?"

Xiaolu explained the legend of Buddha calling a meeting of the animal kingdom but only twelve came, and Buddha honored these animals by naming a year for each of them. "If you're born in the year of the monkey," Xiaolu said, "you're said to be intelligent and successful." He didn't tell them the coming monkey year was predicted to bring disputes into many people's lives.

Ethel said she couldn't have been born in the year of the monkey, and Richard disagreed. "You're smart," he said. "You married me. And look at this place. A real success, something to pass along to these kids."

Kari took Xiaolu's glass from him and set it with hers on the table. "Ready?" She moved toward the kitchen. The boys had gone back to their game; Ricky was tossing a ball down the lane. The ball clamored into the gutter.

Xiaolu went to join his wife in the kitchen. She was leaning over the open oven door, about to pull out the fish. "Wait," he said. "That's not done."

She straightened up. "Aren't we supposed to be eating now?"

He reached past her, shut the oven door. "Let me handle things tonight." He put his hands on her shoulders, tried to steer her away from the stove, but she moved only a step back. "I'll bring out the first course."

"We agreed, nothing elaborate."

"Go sit down and I'll serve everyone. It's the duty of the son-in-law. And while everyone eats, I'll get the second course—"

"That doesn't sound simple." Kari tossed the oven mitt on the counter. "I don't get it. You never wanted to celebrate the Chinese New Year before. Aren't you taking this a little too far?"

He cupped her hands in his; her fingers were cool against his skin. "Please. Allow me." He imagined her pregnant, her body radiating warmth.

She pulled one hand away and reached up to brush a stray hair off his forehead. "But we'll have to interrupt this party when the bowlers arrive." She moved off and when she reached the swinging doors, she turned back and said, "The place does look festive." She flashed him a smile and went out.

For a moment he watched the doors sway, wondering if the whole idea had been a mistake. But he picked up the soup tureen to begin serving his guests. The first course—dried fig, apple and almond soup.

Earlier that morning he had gone to the bowling alley to begin the meal preparations, starting with the dessert. Traditionally, *neen gow* would be made the day before the meal to allow it to cool, but he didn't have that luxury of time. He'd spent the day before cleaning the bowling alley. His ancestors believed sweeping on the New Year was bad luck, and they even kept brooms out of sight. "You don't want to sweep away any good fortune," Auntie Ming had said. And he had never taken any of those warnings seriously before, but now with the uncertainty of his family's future, he thought he should. Yet he knew if Kari asked him about it, she would say it was superstitious and he would have to agree. Silliness. But he wanted to listen, to heed the advice of his ancestors.

Xiaolu had ordered many of the ingredients for this meal from a Chinese market back in Chicago. Nothing like that in the U.P. And he'd found a corner in the bowling alley's pantry to store everything. The alley's kitchen wasn't the best place to prepare a three-course dinner, but the alternative was using Richard and Ethel's. After eight months of living with the in-laws, the alley's kitchen, equipped for short orders, seemed spacious, almost sprawling in comparison. He soaked the red dates in cold water and cut the *peen tong* into pieces, set them in a bowl, and poured boiling water over them. He would have to wait for the dates to soften and for the slabs of brown candy to dissolve and the sugar water to cool.

He was chopping a bell pepper for an omelet when the oilman came in the back door and called out, "Hey, Lou."

"Morning, Pexi." That's what everyone called him, a Finnish nickname; Xiaolu didn't know his real name either.

Pexi asked how Richard and Ethel were doing, and Xiaolu told him Richard was holding his own. Xiaolu wanted to limit the conversation to chitchat; he didn't know the locals well. But the oilman was the first person he was seeing on the New Year, and it would be only proper to offer him breakfast. Start the year off right. But Pexi said Kari had called, asked him to check out the furnace. Xiaolu insisted on scrambling some eggs for them.

"Got any of those famous egg rolls?" Pexi asked. "You probably don't eat them for breakfast, but it's got egg, right? Can't be that bad for you, hey."

Xiaolu didn't want to offend his guest. He told him he'd fire up the deep fryer, and Pexi headed to the basement. Auntie Ming had explained the *yin* and *yang* of nourishment. Too much fried food, she'd told him, wasn't good for you because it was too warming. Keep balance in what you eat, she'd said. And last fall, when it became clear their temporary rearrangement was stretching into the future and he began to feel the need to be busier, to do something useful, to have a role besides devoted husband and stepfather and "not half-bad" son-in-law, Xiaolu had suggested to Kari that they add some Chinese items to the bowling alley's bar menu. "Great idea," she'd said, and he'd considered Auntie Ming's advice and planned accordingly. Steamed dumplings would balance fried dim sum and steamed vegetables would balance chow mein.

But Kari was less enthusiastic about his menu selections. "I want the customers to feel the alley is basically the same," she'd said, "so they keep coming back. I don't want to lose anyone because of the changes."

"It's not a change," he'd said. "It's an addition."

"Okay, how about adding egg rolls and stir fry? Those are familiar."

"I don't want too much fried food."

"But that's what people like," she'd said. "Plus they'll be easy to prep."

And he'd relented, put egg rolls and stir fry on the menu. But he kept the steamed dumplings and vegetables, pointing out their simplicity. At first, he'd ordered bottled sauces and frozen egg rolls and dumplings, but the egg rolls tasted doughy on the inside even when he'd nearly burnt them. Auntie Ming had always made her own, not even using the packaged egg roll wrappers, so he decided to try doing it all from scratch, too. But he didn't have her recipe and had to buy several Chinese cookbooks on-line. He disliked doing this, preferring to leaf through books beforehand, but the area's bookstore, The World of Books, had only one Chinese cookbook, a "quick 'n easy" version. The whole experience made him realize how much he missed browsing through After-Words, his favorite used bookstore in Chicago. When the cookbooks finally arrived, Xiaolu pored through them and tried each egg roll recipe. After several batches that tasted "so-so," he began to improvise; and in between experiments, he read the chapters on traditions and feasts.

By the time Pexi came up from the basement, Xiaolu had breakfast ready. "That furnace will limp along for now," Pexi said. "But it don't look like it'll last another winter."

Xiaolu said he would pass this along to his in-laws, but next winter he expected to be back in Chicago with his family. And if all went well, he would be a father. The limping furnace would not be his concern.

He handed Pexi a plate of egg rolls and steamed peppers and invited him to go up front and sit at the bar. Standing up to eat was no way to start off the New Year.

After Pexi left, he went back to preparing the dessert. The *peen tong* had dissolved and the sugar water was cool, and he added it, slowly, to the rice flour, kneading as he went. As a child, he would help Auntie Ming make the *neen gow*, the dough sticky on his fingers. She would tell him, "To keep our family together. Like these grains of rice, we cling to each other." And she would plop the dough into the soufflé dish and say, "Always a round pan. For unity, life's circle." He would nod and act like he understood because it seemed important to her. But now he thought of her slicing the cake into strips and wondered how that fit together. Cutting the circle. It seemed crucial to understand everything if he was going to be true to the tradition. But he'd missed his chance to learn.

Xiaolu served the soup in crimson bowls he'd bought from the dollar store. The boys came over to take a look, but when he told them what was in the soup, they begged for egg rolls instead. Ethel smiled broadly, the polite look of a tourist, and said the soup sounded interesting, while Richard asked for an egg roll to go with his. Together, Ethel and Kari said, "No fried foods."

"My son-in-law invited me," Richard said, "and he makes the best egg rolls in the whole U.P. Maybe even in this country. That's why you can't jump ship, Lou—"

"Dad, listen. He made this dinner especially for you and Mom. It's a traditional meal. No egg rolls tonight."

"My duty is to my guests," Xiaolu said and headed back to the kitchen. The deep fryer was ready—he'd turned it on earlier because his egg rolls were the most popular item. They'd led to the name change: The Alley had become Egg Roll Alley. It was Ricky's idea. Xiaolu hadn't wanted to change the name—it was putting a stamp on the place, making a claim of sorts—but he didn't argue this with Kari. Instead he pointed out how her parents must feel, having their business taken over, being pushed aside. Too much change for them.

"But they love Ricky's idea," she'd said. "And anyway, it's not a change, it's an addition."

Xiaolu lowered a half-dozen egg rolls into the fryer, and while they cooked, he ate a few spoonfuls of his soup. This had been Auntie Ming's favorite. She'd said it was harmonizing, and that's why he'd picked it for this feast. He turned the egg rolls, tried to relax.

He was setting the egg rolls out to drain when Kari came in carrying the bowls. All three were half-full.

"It was good but maybe not the best choice," she said. "A touch too sweet. They grew up on *mojakka*, that's a stew they understand. Beef and potatoes."

He finished his soup, he wanted to explain everything to his wife, but he knew it would sound like gibberish. He arranged the egg rolls on a platter with small cups of plum sauce (from Yang's Market in Chicago) and spicy soy sauce dip (Auntie Ming's recipe), and Kari took the platter out to her family.

Xiaolu was cutting the Chinese red dates for the *neen gow* after Pexi had left when Ricky came bounding in the back door and declared school had been canceled because it was too cold. This was new to Xiaolu; in all the years he worked as a school counselor, it had never been too cold for classes. Ricky peeled off the layers his grandmother made him wear and piled them on a box in the corner.

Xiaolu asked if he wanted to help and Ricky said, "Yeah, sure." Xiaolu got another knife and showed him how to cut the red dates in half, and when they finished all of them, he got the soufflé dish, the *neen gow* dough already in it.

"You get the important job," Xiaolu said. "The one my Auntie Ming always gave me." He showed Ricky how to place the dates around the outside of the cake, and then had him make a smaller circle in the middle. "For unity," he said, "and for cohesiveness," and Ricky nodded, but Xiaolu recognized the reaction, the same one he'd had as a child. He handed his stepson some white sesame seeds to sprinkle over the top. Then he had Ricky dab vegetable oil on the tips of his fingers. Xiaolu told him to lightly press down the dates and the seeds. "So they stick," he said. "But not too hard. You don't want them to disappear."

When he finished, Ricky swiped his fingers over the sleeve of his sweatshirt and asked if the cake was ready to bake. Xiaolu explained he would have to steam the cake, so Ricky said he was going to play pinball. The alley had two ancient arcade games, both rigged so you didn't need to pay to play. Drop the quarter in and the game started, and the quarter appeared in the coin return. Xiaolu decided the *neen gow* could wait a bit, and he offered a challenge to Ricky. "Loser makes lunch." He knew he wouldn't win.

Xiaolu was putting away the leftover soup when Kari came back into the kitchen and asked if he wanted the last egg roll. He shook his head.

"It's your fault," she said. "You've spoiled them. What's next?"

"*Jai*. Steamed vegetables with rice. Buddhists eat this on the New Year to cleanse the body." She reached over to lift the lid on the rice pot and he pulled her hand away. Foolish to let the *fan hay*, the rice breath escape, but he told her it would make the rice become dry.

"You've become so particular about food," she said. "Could you believe my mom earlier? *The place is bigger or smaller*." Kari giggled and he could smell the sweet wine on her breath. "It's the same."

"She was trying to be polite," he said, but he was thinking about last June when he and Ricky came up. He'd expected Kari to be frazzled, ready to go home. She'd always told him she would never run her own business because she'd seen how hard her parents worked to keep the alley from flaming out. "It's like a baby," she'd said. "A perpetual infant—you're always tied down." But after running the alley for several months, she'd seemed focused and energetic, full of ideas for expansions. She'd told him everything seemed smaller than she remembered. "It's the oddest thing," she'd said, "how different the place is."

Xiaolu lifted the steamer full of vegetables out of the pot, arranged them on a platter, and Kari put the rice in a covered dish. They went back to the table to serve the second course.

Ricky had stood next to the pinball machine, giving pointers— "Not yet, not yet. Now!"—and Xiaolu would pull the lever, the flipper hitting the ball a second too late. "You're not too bummed, are you?" Ricky asked.

"You always beat me. I'm just hoping for a respectable score."

"I meant about not going to Chicago."

For once, Xiaolu hit the ball well, and the lights flashed, metal clicked against metal, the sound muffled, almost weary. "How'd you know I wanted us to go?"

"I heard you and Mom—Go!" But Xiaolu missed the ball. They switched spots, and Ricky started another game. "You guys were, you know, talking."

Her parents lived in a three-bedroom ranch, a place real-estate agents would label "cozy." Hard to keep even ordinary conversations private. Kari and Xiaolu had been "talking." He'd suggested they take some time off, go to Chicago. Once they were out of the U.P., he thought they could talk seriously about their long-term plans: returning home, going back to their real jobs, adding to their family. And they would be able to make love without having to stifle their voices, their noises. No constraints.

But Kari had said, "We can't leave the alley. Dad doesn't have the strength to work and Mom can't do it alone." When Xiaolu had suggested they close it for a few days, she'd said, "You don't understand, Lou. Winter's the busy season. Families stuck together indoors, they need to get out."

"I asked you *not* to call me that," Xiaolu said.

"Sorry, I forget. Everyone else calls you Lou."

"But you're my wife, not *everyone else*."

Later, she told him she'd thought about it some more and suggested he go to Chicago by himself. "I know you miss the city." But he told her he didn't want to be there without her and Ricky. "That's sweet," she'd said and rested her hand on top of his.

They served everyone the second course, Kari spooning a mound of rice on their plates and Xiaolu following behind with the *jai*. He urged them to start eating, told them Chinese restaurants serve the food as it becomes ready because you want to get the *wok hay*, the breath of the wok. If you wait the *wok hay* dissipates. The breath, gone.

But Ethel had one hand linked with Richard's, the other with Ricky's. "We forgot to say grace," she said.

"The breath will last," Kari said. She took her seat and joined hands with her son.

Xiaolu set the platter of *jai* on the table and slipped into the seat next to hers. He reached for her hand and nestled it in his palm. Richard said the prayer and Xiaolu looked around the table. Everyone else had closed their eyes, and Ricky was leaning over his plate with his face down, taking deep breaths. Xiaolu bent his head and did the same, the steam kissing his face.

Earlier that day, he had the big steamer on the stove and was waiting for the water to begin boiling when Kari arrived. She asked where

Ricky was, and he told her he was up front playing pinball.

"Isn't it fun?" she asked. "All of us together on the first day of the Chinese New Year. That wouldn't have happened in Chicago."

"Don't you miss being home?"

She gathered up her son's outerwear, hung it by the door, and said Matt was coming over to hang out with Ricky. Xiaolu told her he would have the boys make some decorations.

"You're going all out for my parents," she said.

He told her it would only be a few things with construction paper and markers. Nothing elaborate. "I have to admit," he said, "that I even miss the traffic on Lake Shore Drive."

She walked over to the stove. "What's in the pot?"

"I'm getting ready to steam the *neen gow*. A traditional dessert for the New Year." He pointed to the soufflé dish on the counter. "A cake."

"You've made this before?"

"My Auntie Ming's recipe."

Kari told him she couldn't wait to try it and walked out of the kitchen. The water was boiling, and Xiaolu lowered the soufflé dish into the steamer, being careful to keep the dish from touching the sides. He covered the steamer, set the timer for thirty-five minutes, and went to join his wife and stepson.

Kari was double-checking the bowling shoes in their cubbyholes, and she frowned at a pair of shoes in her hand before setting them aside.

"Getting this dinner together," he said, "makes me think of our first date." He'd made reservations at a romantic French bistro off the Magnificent Mile. A table for two in the corner, candlelight, and Merlot. They'd made plans to meet there, and while he was waiting for her at the table, Kari called the restaurant. She couldn't make it because Ricky was running a fever.

"I figured I wouldn't get a second chance," she said.

"You shouldn't have been worried. I fell for you right then." It impressed him that she wouldn't leave her son with a babysitter. As a school counselor, he was used to seeing parents put their own desires ahead of their children. Xiaolu had left the bistro, gone to a kosher deli, and bought a quart of chicken noodle soup. He'd dropped by Kari's apartment, and they ate the soup while watching a Cubs game with Ricky.

"I did get worried later." She pulled out another pair of shoes, swapped the mismatched mates with the ones she'd set aside, and slid them back into their correct slots. "Buying Ricky that autographed Sosa baseball—I didn't know what you were thinking. It must have cost an arm and a foot." She grabbed another shoe and waved it at him, grinning.

Xiaolu put his arm around her. "I wanted him to like me."

"I had no doubts. I knew you'd be good with him." She rested her head on his shoulder, and he kissed the top of her head. Her hair was soft and smelled fresh. He imagined their baby would have silky, delicate hair like hers. Kari lifted her face to his, and he kissed her, holding his breath. The two of them pulled apart slowly.

"Sometimes it's important, though," she said, "not to push too hard. Too much and things topple over." She held up the shoe, its lace frayed and broken. "The little things, they get you every time." She headed off in search of a new lace.

Xiaolu began wiping off bowling balls, sticky with sweet-and-sour sauce.

When Matt arrived, the bowling alley filled with the whirlwind of two boys excited at being out of school on a Thursday. They slipped on bowling shoes and slid up and down the lanes. Xiaolu went back to the kitchen and put a kettle on to boil so he could replenish the water in the steamer. Auntie Ming had constantly checked it. "Don't let the water evaporate," she'd said, and he'd asked her how she knew the cake was ready. "I'll show you," and when the time came, she had him peer into the steamer. "See how the cake pulls away from the sides? Then you know."

And one year he asked her how you knew you were "in love," not realizing this was a Western concept, an abstraction. He must have been thirteen or fourteen, and there was a girl with a fierce smile. Auntie Ming had said, "You'll know," and he asked her what you did if you thought you were in love, but the girl ignored you. "Ah, the *yin* and *yang*," she said. "Food, easy to balance. But these other things, much harder. Trust your instincts, your *yin*—" she touched his temple, "and your *yang*." She tapped his breastbone. But he'd wanted something tangible, something he could see, like the sides of the *neen gow* pulling away from the dish.

The kettle whistled and Xiaolu poured more boiling water into the steamer. Kari came in and told him she was going to run some errands. She tugged on her coat and asked him if he needed anything.

"I have everything," he said. "I hope your parents will enjoy the dinner."

"I'm sure they will. Just don't overdo things. We won't have time."

Thursday night was their busiest league night. He'd wanted to have the dinner on the following Sunday, the fourth night of the Chinese New Year, in keeping with tradition. But the Super Bowl was on Sunday, and his mother-in-law was a rabid football fan.

After Kari left, he chopped carrots and red peppers. When the timer finally chimed, he peered into the steamer. The cake was pulling away from the sides. He carefully lifted it out and went to the sink to pour off the excess water.

The boys rushed in, and Ricky asked, "Is the cake ready, Xiaolu?" He cautioned them that it was hot and set it on the counter to cool. They peered at it, and Matt said it didn't look like a cake. Ricky explained it was a Chinese cake and asked Xiaolu if they could have something to eat. He said he'd bring them a snack in a moment, and the boys hurried off.

Xiaolu was opening the double doors, carrying a platter lined with tangerine slices, cashews, and bite-sized Mounds bars, when he heard Matt ask what it was like to have a stepdad who was Chinese.

"He's Chinese-American," Ricky said. "And he wasn't all that different before, in Chicago. He just seems that way here."

Xiaolu stepped back into the kitchen, set the platter down, and took the rack with the *neen gow* to a spot in the pantry. Letting it cool out of the way.

The second course was a success, the platter of *jai* scraped clean. Even the boys had eaten most of theirs, a few unwanted vegetables pushed to the sides of their plates. They were excused from the table and went to bowl. Xiaolu and Kari headed into the kitchen.

He turned the oven off, grabbed the oven mitts, and opened the door, the smell of teriyaki salmon wafting into his face. He pulled out the pan, set it on top of the stove, and removed the foil from the fish. Kari came over to take a look.

"It smells delicious," she said. "And red potatoes, too. Thank you."

Not quite a customary entrée for the New Year. He'd wanted to broil a whole fish in keeping with tradition, but the guy he got the salmon from, an alley regular who used to fish with Richard on Lake Superior, had cut the head off and de-boned it. And the broiler wasn't working; the elements burnt out. Xiaolu sliced the fish, arranged the pieces on a platter with the potatoes, and garnished it with lemon and parsley. Kari took the dish and they went back to the table.

There was little talk at first, the adults busy eating. The salmon was fresh, tender, flaky—perfect—and Xiaolu felt their celebration was getting on track. After the failure of the soup, everything else had gone smoothly. He poured each of them a bit more of the plum wine.

Richard raised his glass and said, "To the cook for a damn good meal." Ethel and Kari chimed in, and they all toasted.

"You really know your way around a kitchen," Ethel said.

"Like I've told you, Lou," Richard said, "the job's yours."

Xiaolu glanced at his wife, but she looked off, past him.

"We talked before about selling," Ethel said. "We knew we wouldn't be able to run the place forever." Her eyes were fixed on the boys as they bowled.

"You never mentioned this to me," Kari said.

"That's because it wasn't serious talk," Richard said and pushed his plate away. "I don't see a problem. Things are rolling along good."

Pins clattered on one of the lanes, and Ricky shouted. "He had a split," Ethel said, "but got the spare." She grabbed her husband's hand. "Remember how Kari stopped bowling when she was a teenager? Said she hated it."

"Yeah," Richard said. "She couldn't wait to get out of here. But I guess you can take the girl out of the bowling alley but not the alley out of the girl." He laughed and leaned over, patted his daughter's arm.

"I think the Atomic Bowlers are here," Kari said. She stood up and walked over to the front entrance, and Xiaolu could hear her greeting people he couldn't see, her voice boisterous.

"The Atomics joke about how they're explosive," Xiaolu said. "But they're at the bottom of the rankings." He tried to smile at this, at his in-laws sitting there, Richard with his arms crossed over his chest, his weak heart, and Ethel tapping her fingers, the telltale sign that she needed a cigarette.

"It's always been this way," she said. "How about dessert?"

Xiaolu rose and began stacking their dinner plates. He told them he had to finish preparing the dessert. Ethel got up and took the salmon platter to the kitchen. Xiaolu came behind with the rest of the dishes.

They piled everything into the sink, and when Ethel began cleaning up, he told her to go back and sit down. But she insisted she needed to keep her hands busy, otherwise she'd have to run out for a smoke. She wouldn't light up in front of her husband. While she scraped leftovers into the garbage can, Xiaolu began loading the dishwasher and she told him stories of the alley before, when there were more people in town and more jobs and more to do.

"During the half-good times we talked about selling," she said. "And during the half-bad times what we talked about was a fire sale. But as Richard said, it was only talk. This place—" She wiped her hands on a towel. "I guess it's part of us, part of the family."

Part of the family. "A baby," Kari had said.

Xiaolu told his mother-in-law he would get the dessert. "A little sweetness for the end of our evening," he said and went to fetch the *neen gow*.

Right before Kari and his in-laws were to arrive for dinner, Xiaolu went to the storage room to check on the *neen gow*. It needed to be cool before being pan-fried, and he was worried he hadn't given it enough time. But the cake was perfect; Auntie Ming would be proud of him. He'd always loved that time in the warm, spice-filled kitchen with her after their New Year's meal. She would cut the cake into quarters, crosswise, creating wide strips, and he would help her cut these strips, crosswise again, into thin slices. While he kept cutting, she would beat an egg, and heat her flat-bottomed wok. "Get it hot," she would say, "but no smoke." She would add a drop of oil to the pan and he would dip the slices of *neen gow* in the egg and add them to the pan in small bunches. "Golden brown," she would say. "That's when they're ready. Serve your guests quick. Best if the slices are hot." And he would sneak one on his way out of the kitchen, and it would burn the roof of his mouth, but he wouldn't care. He liked how the pan-fried slices tasted— sweet, and slightly chewy, like the pieces didn't want to come apart.

Kari came in the kitchen when he was searching for a clean knife to cut the *neen gow*. "Order up," she said. "Dozen egg rolls and two cheeseburgers."

"I was about to get dessert ready."

"You do the orders, I'll take care of dessert."

He found a suitable knife, set it next to the soufflé dish. "It's complicated, I'll have to finish the preparations."

"How complicated can it be? It's a cake."

He pushed the *neen gow* to the back of the counter, out of the way. "It's not ready to eat yet. You pan fry it first."

"Who fries a cake?" She waved her hand at the dish. "Dad's had an egg roll. That's enough. You're the one who's been talking about balance, not eating too much fried food."

"The pieces aren't very big, I doubt one will harm him. It's part of the tradition—" He moved his hands in the air, miming a circle. "A symbol for unity."

She moved over to the freezer, opened it, reached in and grabbed a carton of ice cream, tossed it on the counter, went to the pantry, and came back with a cookie tin. "Mom made chocolate-chip cookies," Kari said. "We can adjust and still be round."

"But the ice cream—"

"Now what's wrong? Vanilla's no good?"

"Ice cream is cold," he said. "The *neen gow*, you eat it hot."

"It's just dessert, nothing more. There won't be any harm in changing the plan."

He moved away, stood to the side as she began digging at the ice cream. Her elbows jerked up and down, and he thought about Ethel and Richard, the two of them talking about a fire sale. He could leave the deep fryer on one night. It might happen, accidents happen. An overheated deep fryer, red-hot sparks balancing the cold, blue-white flames licking the air. But it wouldn't last, the fire would burn itself out and fizzle, and the cold would prevail, and under the wreckage and the ink-charred debris and the ashes, life would be the same. Not bigger, not smaller. The same.

"I was hoping for more."

"You should be happy. Your dinner was fantastic." Kari licked a smear of ice cream off her wrist. "And it was the perfect excuse to get my parents over here, show off how well we're doing." She threw the ice-cream scoop into the sink. It clattered.

"Pexi was here this morning," he said. "You'll have to replace the furnace before next winter. He says it won't last." Xiaolu could see it straining to pump out more heat, the overworked pieces breaking apart, scattering. Its breath, gone.

"That's a great start to the new year," Kari said, turning around, a plate full of ice-cream sandwiches in her hand. "I'll bring these out to the boys and Mom. Later, after we close up, we can have some of that cake. Just the two of us." She walked off, the doors swinging behind her.

Xiaolu cut the *neen gow* into quarters and sliced those into thin strips and beat an egg in a bowl. He heated the flat-bottomed wok, the one handed down from Auntie Ming, and poured a drop of oil into the wok. He held his hand over it until he felt his palm begin to sweat and then began frying small batches before the oil could begin to smoke. When the first pieces were ready, he arranged them on a platter and rushed out to the table.

"My gift to you," he said, presenting the platter first to his in-laws, his honorary guests. "A traditional dessert for the Chinese New Year."

Ethel took a piece and told him she would share it with Richard. The boys had gone off to bowl so Xiaolu turned to his wife and offered her a slice, the platter cradled in his outstretched hands.

"I don't have room for anything else," she said and moved off.

Xiaolu stood still, the breath of the wok escaping into the cold air. From across the alley, he heard the crash of pins struck by a ball.

Angela Vogel

MIGRAINEUR

"Is it pounding or pulsing?" the doctor asks, and I say, "Neither.
Or both," because I am not really sure what pulsing and pounding
    feels like
objectively, and since he is hitting me with French descriptive words
like *common* and *classic* and *migraineur*, I start checking random
    "yeses"
on the form before he volunteers that he has not seen this occurrence
occur after forty. We are sitting in an office designed by architects to
    be easy
on the eye since that's one of the big three: aura, stomach upset, and
    sound—
and while it's dim behind my sunglasses, it's tough to ignore the devil
I know beading at my skull, so I guess the genesis of my problem
is current events, to which he says Ah, you are stressed then, to which
    I reply Yes,
Jackass, only I don't say that last part out loud, because I try not to
    curse publicly,
especially to the guy with his hand up my back trying to stop the bell
    in my brain.
He says he can prescribe a preventive and wants to know what I do
    for a living, and I say teach
English and creative writing courses online, why do you ask?
    and he says because
this med's biggest side effect is stupidity, and I say, so if I were a
    model
or rodeo clown this drug would be OK, but taking it now would be
    akin
to administering Kerouac lithium, right? and he says he doesn't know
    if Kerouac

took lithium but he definitely didn't take *this* drug because it's too
  new.
Later my sister says those must be some God-awful headaches to risk
  stupidity,
and I think of all the game show contestants who selected what
was behind curtain number three when curtains one and two offered
  really good
options only to walk away with squat. *Do consolation prizes console?*
  seems a less
pressing query now than *Are the dumb numb to what dumbs them?*
  Still, one lost job
plus three kids divvied by divorce equals one splitting headache in the
  show-
your-work column, and Medusa in my duvet isn't metaphor enough
to describe what awaits me in morning, which by now should be
  soon enough
to figure the drug company's not the only one sitting pretty.

Jason Lee Brown

WHY MR. PRESIDENT LOVES SOAP BUBBLES

They [the iridescent colors of soap bubbles]
are not the same as rainbow colors
but are the same as the colors in an oil slick.

—*Wikipedia*

It's not for the science. The Decider
has no time
                    for complex thoughts
of mathematical properties, his hazel eyes
twitching side to side (as if failing
a sobriety test) at the thin, filmed sphere
of soap water
                    floating aimlessly
as the first thirty-five years of his life.

It's not for the scepter,
                    a plastic yellow wand
he unsheathes from the clear solution,
his thin lips pursed, blowing, O,
as if in the middle of saying the word hope,

but it's for this:
                    he loves the anticipation
of the pop! that ends it all
                    when he cups
the miniature iridescent earth in his palm
and bites down,
                    giggling as the solution
bursts on his tongue, leaving nothing
but the bitter aftertaste of dispensation.

CONTRIBUTORS' NOTES

Jürgen Becker is the author of over thirty books—novels, story collections, poetry collections, and plays—all published by Germany's premier publisher, Suhrkamp. He has won numerous prizes in Germany, including the Heinrich Böll Prize, the Uwe Johnson Prize, and the Hermann Lenz Prize, among others.

Mark D. Bennion has taught writing and literature courses at Brigham Young University-Idaho for the past seven years. In 2000, he graduated with an M.F.A. from the University of Montana. Recently his poems have appeared in *The Comstock Review*, *Irreantum*, and *Animus*, and forthcoming in *caesura*, *Aurorean*, and *Dialogue: A Journal of Mormon Thought*. Mark and his wife, Kristine, are the parents of three daughters.

Jessica M. Brophy is currently writing her English Ph.D. dissertation at Morgan State University. She has been published in the *Greenwood Encylopedia of African American Women Writers* and *Burning Leaf*, and forthcoming work will appear in the *Cherry Blossom Review* and *Literary Horizons*. She also teaches writing at Villa Julie College in Stevenson, MD and enjoys walking, letter writing, and collecting earrings.

Jason Lee Brown teaches analytical writing at Southern Illinois University Carbondale, where he lives with his wife Haruka. His work has appeared in *The Journal*, *Spoon River Poetry Review*, *Post Road*, *Ecotone* and others. He was recently nominated for Pushcart Prizes in fiction and poetry and just finished co-editing the anthology *Best of the Midwest: Fresh Writing from Twelve States* with Shanie Latham.

Teri Ellen Cross has an M.F.A. from American University and is a Cave Canem fellow. Her poems have appeared in several anthologies and journals including *Bum Rush the Page: a Def Poetry Jam*, *Gathering Ground: A Reader Celebrating Cave Canem's First Decade*, *Beltway Poetry Quarterly*, *Torch*, and the upcoming summer issue of *Gargoyle*. She lives in Silver Spring, MD.

John Michael Cummings' short stories have appeared in more than seventy-five literary journals, including *North American Review*, *Alaska Quarterly Review*, and *The Iowa Review*, and forthcoming in *The Kenyon Review*. He has been twice nominated for *The Pushcart Prize*. His debut novel, *The Night I Freed John Brown*, is scheduled to be published by Penguin in May of 2008.

Stephanie Dickinson lives in New York City. Her work appears in *Cream City Review*, *Green Mountains Review*, *African-American Review*, and *Chelsea*, among others. Rain Mountain Press, a publishing collective, recently released her book of short stories, *Road of Five Churches* and *Corn Goddess*, a poetry collection. "Pig farmer's Stepfather" received a distinguished story citation in *Best American 2007 Short Stories*.

Okla Elliott is currently an M.F.A. student at Ohio State University and also holds an M.A. from UNC-Greensboro. His nonfiction, poetry, short fiction, and translations appear in such journals as *Blue Mesa Review, Cold Mountain Review, International Poetry Review, North Dakota Quarterly*, and *Sewanee Theological Review*. He is the author of *The Mutable Wheel* and *Lucid Bodies and Other Poems*.

Kim Foster's work has appeared previously in *Curve* and *Bellevue Literary Review*, among other publications. An avid reader of Southern literature, she lives near Atlanta and is at work on a novel.

Charles R. Gillespie lives in Imperial, Texas.

Karen Hildebrand grew up in Colorado and, after spending a few years in San Francisco, now lives in NYC where she works in magazine publishing. Her poetry has appeared or is forthcoming in a number of journals and she blogs about life in NYC on her website.

Claire Ibarra was a Montessori teacher for ten years but has been writing stories since she can remember. She and her husband own a hostel in the Andes Mountains of Peru, which is the setting for the current novel she's writing. When Claire is not traveling in Peru, she's taking creative writing classes and raising a family in Miami, FL.

Luisa A. Igloria is an Associate Professor at Old Dominion University. Luisa has published 9 books including *Encanto* (Anvil, 2004), In The Garden of The Three Islands (Moyer Bell/Asphodel, 1995), and most recently Trill & Mordent (WordTech Editions, 2005). Trill & Mordent was nominated for the 9th annual Library of Virginia Literary Awards in 2006, and received a 2007 Global Filipino Literary Award.

Deb Jurmu is a transplanted "Yooper" now living in Bethesda, MD where she works for the Cystic Fibrosis Foundation. She received her M.F.A. from Southern Illinois University, Carbondale in May 2006. This is her second appearance in *Natural Bridge*.

David Dodd Lee is the author of the forthcoming book of poems, *Automatic Thank You Kisses*, (Four Way Books, 2009). He is also the author of four previous books of poems, including *Abrupt Rural* (New Issues, 2004), and he is the editor of *SHADE*, an anthology of poetry and fiction. He has recently completed a book of Ashbery Erasure poems. And new stories have appeared in *Green Mountains Review* and *Controlled Burn*.

Nathan Leslie's six books of fiction include *Madre, Reverse Negative*, and *Drivers*. Nathan's stories, essays, and poems have appeared in over 100 literary magazines including *Boulevard, Shenandoah, North American Review*, and *Cimarron Review*. He is fiction editor for *The Pedestal Magazine* and series editor for the forthcoming Dzanc Books' *The Best of the Web 2007* anthology.

Keming Liu is an Associate Professor at Medgar Evers College of the City University of New York where she teaches literature, linguistics, and composition. She is also a guest professor at Long Island University's C.W. Post campus where she lectures on Chinese literature and the arts. Liu holds a doctoral degree in linguistics from Columbia University's Teachers College.

Aimee Loiselle writes fiction in Minnesota, but she is a New Englander who gets cranky if she can't feel the ocean. Her stories have appeared in *Square Lake* and *Out of Line*, and her novel manuscript was short-listed for the 2007 Faulkner-Wisdom Competition. She currently mentors a high school student in Minneapolis and often nags him to read aloud.

Bridget Meeds' long poem "Light" was published in *Wild Workshop* (Faber and Faber, UK, 1997) and in *American Poetry Review*. Her poems have appeared or are forthcoming in *Witness, Seneca Review,* and *Dos Passos Review*. She has published full-length books *Audience* (2007) and *Tuning the Beam* (2000) with Vista Periodista.

Julia Older's translations of *Blues For A Black Cat And Other Stories* by Boris Vian were published by the University of Nebraska Press in 2001 and by Rupa Co in New Delhi, India in 2005. Her tenth poetry book, *Tahirih Unveiled* was published by Turning Point in 2007. Older's essays, poems, and translations have appeared in *Poets & Writers, Entelechy International, The New Yorker, New Letters* and other publications.

Jan Pettit was raised in a disappearing Nebraska town. She now lives and writes in Minneapolis, MN. Her poetry has appeared in *Great River Review, South Dakota Review, Rosebud Magazine, Tusculum Review* and in *Nebraska Presence,* an anthology of poets from Nebraska. She is currently working on a book of prose and poetry titled *Nebraska: Excerpts from a Small Town.*

Zach Savich has had recent poems in and accepted by *Kenyon Review, Jubilat, American Letters and Commentary,* and other journals. He currently teaches at Kirkwood Community College.

Eric Paul Shaffer's fiction appears in *Bakunin, Bamboo Ridge, Cutting Edge Quarterly,* and *Prose Ax. Burn & Learn,* his first novel, will be published in 2008. He is also author of five books of poetry, including *Lāhaina Noon, Living at the Monastery, Working in the Kitchen,* and *Portable Planet*. His poetry appears in *Ploughshares, Slate, North American Review, Threepenny Review,* and elsewhere.

Carrie Shipers received her M.F.A. from The Ohio State University. Recent poems have appeared in *Crab Orchard Review, Barrow Street, Sow's Ear Poetry Review, Mid-American Review,* and other journals. Her chapbook *Ghost-Writing* was recently released by Pudding House. She is currently a Ph.D. student at the University of Nebraska-Lincoln.

Joanna Sit is a poet who lives in Brooklyn. Her work has appeared recently in *Pegasus, Fickle Muses,* and *Poem*. She teaches Composition at Medgar Evers College of the City University of New York.

Ryan Stone earned his M.F.A. from UM–St. Louis in 2004. His fiction has appeared in *Natural Bridge* ("Hotel Carnival," no. 4), *Wisconsin Review*, and the anthology *Under the Arch: St. Louis Stories*. He teaches writing at Missouri State University–West Plains.

Boris Vian (1920-1959) has been called a novelist, playwright, librettist, essayist, jazz critic, trumpeter, engineer, inventor, songwriter, singer, actor, poet, and a few names not fit for print. He frequented jazz caves with Edith Piaf and Simone de Beauvoir and translated American noir mysteries for friend and Gallimard editor Jean Paul Sartre, who nominated Vian's novel for the French Pleiade Award mentioned in "The Priest in Swim Trunks."

Angela Vogel's poems have appeared in *POOL*, *Barrow Street*, *Southern Poetry Review*, *Valparaiso Poetry Review*, *RHINO*, and *Pebble Lake Review*, and forthcoming in *The National Poetry Review*. She is a 2004 Pushcart Prize nominee, and her chapbook, *Social Smile*, was published in 2004 by Finishing Line Press. She teaches creative writing at Florida Community College at Jacksonville and publishes *New Zoo Poetry Review*.

Valerie Vogrin is the author of a novel, *Shebang* (University Press of Mississippi). Her stories have appeared in journals such as *Black Warrior Review*, *Chattahoochee Review*, *New Orleans Review*, and *The Florida Review*. She is an Assistant Professor at Southern Illinois University Edwardsville and prose editor of *Sou'wester*.

Yu Xiang (b. 1970) lives in Ji'nan, Shandong Province. Yu received an award from China's "Poetry Monthly" for its eleventh annual poetry contest in China.

Claire Zoghb's work has appeared in *Yankee*, *Connecticut Review*, *CALYX*, *Saranac Review*, *Mizna: Prose, Poetry and Art Exploring Arab America*, *Natural Bridge* and *Through A Child's Eyes* (an anthology on children and war). A Pushcart nominee, Claire has been awarded honors from the Rita Dove Poetry Prize and Dogwood. She lives in New Haven, where she is a freelance graphic artist and book designer.

Natural Bridge would like to acknowledge the following individuals and organizations for their invaluable support:

FRIENDS OF NATURAL BRIDGE

Pierre Davis
Delmar Literary Journal
Gene W. Doty
Ross Gay
Varda T. Haimo
Anne Hinds
X. J. Kennedy
Christine T. Portell
Mary Troy

ST. LOUIS LITERARY LIGHTS

Anne Earney
Mary Kaye Fort
Gianna Jacobson
Alvin L. Siwak
Stacy Siwak
Arnold Traubitz
John C. Van Doren

Natural Bridge

Back Issues are $5 unless otherwise noted.
Send a check or money order to:

Natural Bridge Back Issues
Department of English
University of Missouri-St. Louis
One University Blvd.
St. Louis, MO 63121

or online at http://www.fictionondemand.com

Number 1, Spring 1999: Our inaugural issue includes work by Bob Hicok, Sandra Kohler, Greg Pape, Jennifer Atkinson, Leslie Pietrzyk, Jim Daniels, and Akos Fodor; new translations of Wang Wei & Xi Murong; and also featuring 10 contemporary Hungarian poets translated by Michael Castro & Gábor G. Gyukics.

Number 10, Fall 2003: Guest-edited by Jeff Friedman. Includes work by Chard deNiord, Ken Smith, Richard Newman, Joan Larkin, Tess Gallagher, Attila Joseph, and Kevin Prufer.

Number 2, Fall 1999: Includes work by Lee Upton, Jeff Friedman, Diane Wakoski, Rita Ciresi, Nancy Zafris, and Jeff Hamilton.

Number 11, Spring 2004: Fiction Issue, edited by Mary Troy. New works by Lex Williford, Jaimee Wriston Colbert, Jacob Appel, C.D. Albin, Michael Prtichett, Jane O. Wayne, and Jeff Friedman. [$8.00, limited quantity]

Number 3, Spring 2000: Kevin Boyle, Sarah Browning, Eric Pankey, Laura Jensen, Donald Finkel, Cesare Pavese, Jennifer Atkinson, and Kent Shaw.

Number 12, Fall 2004: Edited by Steven Schreiner. Features work by Cecily Idding, Lisa Ampleman, Carl Dennis, Jeff Friedman, Adam Berlin, Franz Kafka, and more.

Number 4, Fall 2000: Short Story feature, edited by Mary Troy. Fiction by Catherine Brady,.John Griswold, Ian MacMillan, Charles Wyatt , Ian MacMillian, an essay by Katheryn Gessner, a translation by Chang Chi, and more.

Number 13, Spring 2005: Diaspora Issue, edited by Eamonn Wall. Features work by Elizabeth Huergo, Claudette Mork Sigg, Debra L. Cumberland, Jacob M. Appel, Joseph Lennon, and more.

Number 5, Spring 2001: Long Poem feature, edited by Steven Schreiner. Work by Christopher Buckley, Rebecca Dunham, Peter Streckfus, Naomi Shihab Nye, Baron Wormser, George Keithley, and Göran Sonnevi.

Number 14, Fall 2005: Features fragment and sequence, edited by Ruth Ellen Kocher. Features work by Timothy Liu, Brian Turner, Beckian Fritz Goldberg, Ross Gay, Sapphire, Tayari Jones, Kent Annan, and many more.

Number 6, Fall 2001: Highlighting the essay, edited by David Carkeet. A.E. Hotchner, John Dalton, Harry Mark Petrakis, William J. Cobb, Mark Johnston, David Salner, Brian Doyle, and Roger Hart.

Number 15, Spring 2006: Dreams Issue, edited by Howard Schwartz. Features work by Marvin Bell, Gerald Stern, Joy Harjo, K. Curtis Lyle, Majorie Stelmach, Arthur Sze, and more. [no longer available]

Number 7, Spring 2002: Special Irish Issue, edited by Eamonn Wall. New work by Kevin Boyle, Michael Coady, Greg Delanty, Tyler Farrell, Ray McManus, Mary O'Donoghue, Geri Rosenzweig, Daniel Tobin, X.J. Kennedy and others. [$8.00]

Number 16, Fall 2006: Writers Responding to Women Writers Issue, edited by Nanora Sweet. Features work by A. E. Stallings, Sandra Gilbert, Catherine Rankovic, Lee Upton, and more.

Number 8, Fall 2002: Short Fiction feature, guest-edited by Lex Williford. Featuring work by Dan Pope, Jonis Agee, Alison Joseph, Wendy Bishop, Gaylord Brewer and R.T. Smith.

Number 17, Spring 2007: New & Emerging Writers Issue, edited by John Dalton. Features work by Ron Savage, Elyse Fenton, Sandra Kohler, Jack Garrett, Evan Morgan Williams, Jennifer Merrifield, and more.

Number 9, Spring 2003: Special Genesis Issue, edited by Howard Schwartz. Features Donald Finkel, Jason Sommer, Ira Cohen, Michael Castro, Steve Stern, and others. [$8.00]

Number 18, Fall 2007: Temptation Issue, edited by Steven Schreiner. Features work by Charles Baxter, Bob Hicok, David Clewell, Denise Duhamel, Eric Pankey, and more.